P7-CHC-205

STATEMENT FOR AUTHORS SUBMITTING MSS TO PADS

The object of the American Dialect Society, as stated in its constitution, "is the study of the English language in North America, together with other languages influencing it or influenced by it." The Society is therefore interested in publishing in its journal *Publication of the American Dialect Society (PADS)* studies by its members in (1) regional dialects, (2) social dialects, (3) occupational vocabulary, (4) place names, (5) usage, (6) non-English dialects, (7) new words, (8) proverbial sayings, and (9) the literary use of dialect. Models for these kinds of studies may be found in earlier issues of *PADS*.

PADS does not publish articles on general grammar without dialect emphasis or articles on literary figures not known as dialect writers.

The general policy of *PADS* is to devote each issue to two or three long articles, or, more commonly, to a single study of monograph length. Shorter articles aimed at a relatively general readership of diverse interests should be submitted to *American Speech*, edited by Ronald Butters, Duke University.

Any MS submitted to *PADS* should be styled by the MLA *Style Sheet* (2nd ed., 1970) and accompanied by a one-paragraph abstract of not over 200 words prepared by the "Guidelines" printed in *PMLA*, Vol. 83, No. 2 (May 1968). Forms are obtainable from the Editor.

PADS does not publish book reviews.

It is the Editor's policy to acknowledge the receipt of articles promptly, and the policy of the Editing Committee to accept or reject them within six months.

PUBLICATION
OF THE
AMERICAN
DIALECT
SOCIETY

NUMBER 69

GOING NATIVE: THE REGENERATION OF SAXON ENGLISH

DENNIS E. BARON
University of Illinois

PUBLISHED FOR
THE SOCIETY BY
UNIVERSITY OF
ALABAMA PRESS
UNIVERSITY, ALABAMA

LIBRARY
The University of Texas
At San Antonio

PREFACE

Oliver Pritchett, writing in a recent issue of the magazine *Europe*, notes the latest in a long series of examples of English francophobia. The British House of Commons, it seems, has "ordained that the menu in the dining room used by Members of Parliament should no longer be printed in French. The plain food with which parliamentarians sustain themselves must be now described in plain English. *Consommé* is now 'clear soup' and that is that. Indeed, the reform is so revolutionary and sweeping that the words 'French fried' are banned. Henceforth the correct terminology is 'chips.'" Pritchett attributes the change to a new pride in English cooking. He quotes Liberal MP Clement Freud: "It is shameful having *'le roast beef avec le Yorkshire pudding'* on the menu.... There is no good reason why an English meal cooked by a Chinese and served by an Italian should be given a French name" (July-August 1981, p. 15).

Opinions of English food aside, a significant number of writers over the past four hundred years have felt that the English language has borrowed too much of its vocabulary from other tongues. Even today, when the balance of lexical trade appears to have shifted, and English seems to be exporting more terms than it is taking in, an occasional outcry against the French or classical elements of our vocabulary can be heard. While most critics of the English language are content to permit borrowings that fill a demonstrated need and that can be nativized to fit English pronunciation and morphology, a few have objected to the presence of any word that cannot trace its ancestry back to Anglo-Saxon or a cognate Germanic language. Some would go so far as to uproot borrowed words, replacing them with already existing native ones or new words coined on Anglo-Saxon principles of word formation.

A few studies of English linguistic history have commented on the movement to eradicate borrowed words in the Renaissance and in the later nineteenth century, but the present work is the first attempt to trace the Saxonist movement from its origins in the late 1500s to the present day. A number of people have given me valuable assistance in the preparation of this monograph, and I would like to thank them publicly here. The manuscript was read by Iryce Baron, James Hartman, and Joseph B. Trahern, Jr. (himself a native speaker of West Saxon), all of whom made many useful suggestions for its improvement. I have tried to follow their recommendations whenever possible, although any errors of fact and infelicities of style remain my own. Professor J.J. Campbell led me to the work of Martin Tupper. Anne Schmidt, my tireless research assistant, helped me with bibliography and the checking of references and saved me from the embarrassment of referring to Jessie M. Anderson as a man. The librarians at the University of Illinois have been both generous with their time and imaginative in their efforts to procure for me copies of some rather obscure texts. Finally I should like to thank the members of the American Dialect Society, so many of whom have encouraged me in this and several other projects over the past few years. It is to them that I dedicate this book.

Urbana, Illinois
October, 1981

CONTENTS

1. THE RENAISSANCE

About 450 years after the Norman conquest of Britain, users of the English language began feeling uncomfortable about its extensive borrowings from French and the classical languages, Latin and Greek. From the sixteenth to the twentieth centuries, some writers have seen English as a primitive and impoverished tongue that was forced to swell its vocabulary with foreign imports from more cultured climes in order to express effectively the innovations and complexities of modern life. Most commentators on the English language have accepted and even celebrated its ability to absorb new words and adapt to new linguistic influences, treating the huge English word-hoard as a treasure to be protected and nourished. But others, viewing all borrowing as a harmful dilution of the ancient Saxon purity of English, have sought at various times to rescue the language from the undue influence of the French, the Papists, the Greek and Latin scholars, the culture-famished middle classes, the mad scientists and technocrats, or the free-lance neologists, all of whom created new words on non-English models with alarming and irreverent abandon.

Most critics of borrowing were content to caution English speakers and writers against the dangers of excess. They warned of the possible disappearance of English: if borrowing were to continue at its present pace, they contended, our children would need dictionaries of Latin or French in order to understand their native speech. Many advised a return to a simpler and plainer English, free from figured language, ornate diction and obvious foreign imports, though not necessarily free from the many borrowed words that had been nativized over the centuries and that had become an integral part of the language. Such an idea is no doubt behind the decision, recounted in Thomas Sprat's *History of the Royal Society* (London, 1667), to avoid "extravagant" speech and "swellings of style" in scientific writing, "to return back to the primitive purity, and shortness, when men deliver'd so many *things*, almost in an equal number of *words*. [The Royal Society] have exacted from all their members, a close, naked, natural way of speaking; positive expressions; clear senses; a native easiness: bringing all things as near the Mathematical plainness, as they can: and preferring the language of Artizans, Countrymen, and Merchants, before that, of Wits, or Scholars" (p. 113).

But in the sixteenth and seventeenth centuries, and again in the nineteenth and twentieth, a few reformers tried to purge English of some or all of its nonnative vocabulary, and to replace the ousted words with what we may call Saxonisms. There are three basic types of words that are defined here as Saxonisms: revivals of long-discarded Anglo-Saxon terms; provincialisms which were thought to preserve the original Old English unmixed and undefiled; and new coinages based on Anglo-Saxon or other Germanic analogies, to be used generally when no words of the first or second type were available to fill a semantic gap. Saxonism has sometimes been defined as plainness of speech in contrast to ornate or inflated diction. Indeed, the Royal Society might have so defined it in the seventeenth century. However it will become apparent that, despite the intentions of their proponents, the Saxonisms discussed in this monograph have as their effect anything but plainness. They are often strange, unusual, or archaic words that strike the reader as foreign and difficult. They do not have the quality of transparency that we associate with the plain style, and although many of them are certainly native terms, they have the appearance of wayward exiles.

William Tyndale and John Cheke raised some eyebrows by employing a few Saxonisms in their sixteenth century translations of the Bible into the vernacular. Ralph Lever (1573) and Nathaniel Fairfax (1674) used Saxonisms extensively in their respective works on logic and metaphysics. And in the period between 1870 and 1917 William Barnes, Elias Molee, and Charles Louis Dessoulavy made Saxonism the basis for their own linguistic reforms. Even today some writers on the English language distinguish the Saxon from the classical elements of its vocabulary, advising the use of one or the other, or a mixture of both, as occasion demands, and we still occasionally hear calls in the public press for a return to language reminiscent of a purer, simpler time, for example the suggestion in the *New Statesman* that *escalator* be replaced by the "native" *upgangflow*.[1]

SAXONISM IN THE RENAISSANCE

In the Renaissance in England, antique and Latinate diction were sometimes lumped together as a single rhetorical vice, called by Samuel Daniel "this idle affectation of antiquitie or noueltie," although it was clear to most writers that the vice lay not in using either archaic or inkhorn terms but in overusing them. As George Gascoigne notes in 1575, foreign terms could sometimes be highly effective: "Eschew straunge words, or *obsoleta et inusitata*, vnlesse the Theame do giue iust occasion: marie, in some places a straunge worde doth drawe attentiue reading."[2] Users of inkhorn terms, on the other hand, often scorned the monosyllabic Saxon base of English and called for its embellishment. Defending his own use of such ornate inkhornisms as *mummianized, preludately, cloyance, collachrimate, gardent*, and *plangorous*, Thomas Nashe writes in 1594 that these "are not halfe so harsh in their definence as the old hobbling English verbes." Nashe finds the native English word stock impoverished:

Our English tongue of all languages most swarmeth with the single money of monasillables which are the onely scandall of it. Bookes written in them and no other, seeme like Shop-keepers boxes, that containe nothing else, saue halfepence, three-farthings and two pences. Therefore what did me I, but hauing a huge heape of those worthlesse shreds of small English in my *Pia maters* purse to make the royaller shew with them to mens eyes, had them to the compounders immediately, and exchanged them foure into one, and others into more, according to the Greek, French, Spanish, and Italian.[3]

Sir Philip Sidney recognizes that English is a "mingled language" and approves of this fact, objecting only to excessive ornamentation in writing. Sidney praises the Saxon element in English which, unlike the French, Latin, or even German, is "so voyd of those cumbersome differences of Cases, Genders, Moodes, and Tenses, which I thinke was a peece of the Tower of *Babilons* curse, that a man should be put to schoole to learne his mothertongue."[4] George Puttenham is aware of the Saxon heritage of English and of Saxon survivals in certain localized dialects of sixteenth century English speech, but in *The Arte of English Poesie* (1589) he proposes for his linguistic standard the usage of the court and of the areas within a sixty-mile radius of London, not the language of the provinces, particularly the North, which was seen as the most conservative: "Though no man can deny but that theirs is the purer English Saxon at this day, yet it is not so Courtly nor so currant as our Southerne English." Puttenham also rejects the dialect of port cities, where foreign terms are too likely to gain admittance, and the speech of preachers, schoolmasters, or universities, "where Schollers vse much peeuish affectation of words out of the primatiue languages," in other words, where inkhorn terms are likely to abound. Puttenham maintains a balanced view. He approves of borrowing when there is no suitable English equivalent available, and he points to such useful imports as *scientificke, maior-domo, politien, conduict, idiome,* and *significative.* But he values native words as well. Puttenham finds *sauvage* better than the Saxon *wilde,* and *obscure* better than *dark,* but he does not like *audacious* as a substitute for *bold,* or *compatible* for the nativized *agreeable in nature* (*Elizabethan Critical Essays,* 2:150-53).

Richard Carew sees borrowing as a natural and unavoidable linguistic phenomenon. In his *Epistle on the Excellency of the English Tongue* (?1595-96) he says, "So the Greekes robbed the Hebrewes, the Latins the Greeks...and (in a manner) all other Christian Nations the Latine." In fact Carew feels that the borrowing of words can actually revitalize them: "We employ the borrowed ware so farre to our aduantage that we raise a profit of new words from the same stocke, which yet in their owne countrey are not merchantable." Carew finds that a mixed English is a harmonious one, although he takes special care to commend our native Saxon monosyllables and such concise, self-explaining Saxon compounds as *handkercher, wisdom,* and *doomsday.*[5] William Camden agrees with Carew that our borrowed words are valuable, for they have made of English a language as good as any in Europe, and he too admires the ancient English-Saxon roots which give the language an unmatched efficiency. In Camden's *Remaines Concerning Britain* (1614), which also contains Carew's *Epistle,* he says, "As for the *Monosyllables* so rife in our tongue, which were not so originally, although they are vnfitting for verses and measures, yet are they most fit for expressing briefly the first conceipts of the minde...so that we can set downe more matter in fewer lines, then any other language."[6]

William L'Isle, a pioneer in Anglo-Saxon studies who in 1638 published an edition of the writings of Aelfric, also approves of the present state of English, finding it an improved and dexterous tongue, and not a "mingle-mangle." Nonetheless L'Isle recommends the study of Anglo-Saxon partly to help us understand our past and partly to discourage unnecessary imports. Discussing the Anglo-Saxon vocabulary he says, "I wish not this to the end we should againe call this old garbe into vse; but to hold where we are without borrowing when we need not."[7] And lexicographer Edward Phillips, nephew of John Milton, states in his *New World of English Words* (1658) that borrowing can be beneficial as well as harmful, although he makes a special case for the retention of Saxon monosyllables: "If that sentence be judged most praiseworthy that containeth most matter in fewest words, why may we not commend that word, which consisting of fewest syllables, is yet of as great force as if it had more." Similarly Phillips finds that our native compounds, "words which are produced by the coalition, or clapping together of two of these monosyllables into one, as the word *wisdome*," are as expressive as borrowed polysyllables.[8] Phillips does not care for Spenser's archaisms, and he feels that a mixed English is a smoother one, but he also clearly admires the endurance of Saxon English: "The Saxon words...cannot be counted so obsolete as some would have them." And his comment on the present independence of English suggests a belief that we have already borrowed enough: "It is our happinesse that being a terror to other nations, we are now free from invaders that formerly altred our Language" (D1^v).

In the *Epistle Dedicatory to the Shepheards Calender* (1579), E.K. defends Edmund Spenser's use of archaic words in several ways. For one thing, he finds archaic language to be stylistically appropriate for shepherds. It makes Spenser's rhymes "more ragged and rustical" and it gives them both authority and grace: "Such olde and obsolete wordes are most vsed of country folke." E.K. cites Tully's dictum that "ofttimes an auncient worde maketh the style seeme graue," and he argues that the occasional archaism only sets off the beauty of the fancier words: "Euen so doe those rough and harsh termes enlumine, and make more clearly to appeare, the brightnesse of braue and glorious words." And finally E.K. praises Spenser as a conservator of the language: "He hath laboured to restore, as to theyr rightfull heritage, such good and naturall English words as haue ben long time out of vse and almost cleane disherited." Others who have tried to remedy the loss of our old words by borrowing or neologizing have only botched the job: "They patched up the holes with peces and rags of other languages.... So now they haue made our English tongue a gallimaufray or hodgepodge of al other speches."[9]

Richard Verstegan, a Catholic who moved to Antwerp and published and sent religious literature to England, presents in 1605 an account of the history of the English language and calls for a reversal of its present patterns of borrowing and word formation, a position more common among Protestant writers. Verstegan comments on the great antiquity of the language, tracing it back to the tower of Babel because the word *babble* in English means 'confusion of speech.' He cites, although he does not claim to believe it, the controversial argument of Johannes Goropius Becanus, physician to Queen Mary of Hungary, that English was the oldest of the world's tongues and had been spoken in Paradise. Becanus saw in the name *Adam* the word *atem* 'breath,' while in *Eve* he found *even* 'the same.' In *Cain* Becanus found *keen* 'angry, shrewd;' and in *Abel* he read *able* 'one that is sufficient.' Verstegan feels that English simply fitted itself to these ancient names, and he sees in the connections between *God* and *good,* and *devil* and *evil,* additional support for this opinion. Verstegan posits a Teutonic ancestor for modern English and further argues that all the Germanic languages including Frankish, or French, were at one time identical. English has strayed from its origins more than the other members of the family, but according to Verstegan a letter written in unmixed English would be so like the Dutch that it could be understood both in England and in Holland.

Verstegan holds the common Renaissance view that Chaucer was responsible for the large number of French terms in English, "for that hee was descended of French or rather wallon race." But Verstegan finds that the borrowing process has gotten out of hand:

Since the tyme of *Chaucer,* more Latin & French, hath bin mingled with our toung then left out of it, but of late wee haue falne to such borowing of woords from, Latin, French, and other toungs, that it had bin beyond all stay and limit, which albeit some of vs do lyke wel and think our toung thereby much bettred, yet do strangers therefore carry the farre lesse opinion thereof, some saying that it is of it self no language at all, but the scum of many languages, others that it is most barren, and that wee are dayly faine to borrow woords for it (as though it yet lacked making) out of other languages to patche it vp withall, and that yf wee were put to repay our borrowed speech back again, to the languages that may lay claime vnto it; wee should bee left little better then dumb, or scarsly able to speak any thing that should bee sencible.

Verstegan feels that when words are borrowed they lose their original meanings, "and therefore as wel may we fetch woords from the Ethiopians, or East or West Indians, and thrust them into our language and baptise all by the name of English, as those which wee dayly take from the Latin, or languages thereon depending." Furthermore, one effect of so much foreign influence on

English is that Englishmen are having increasing difficulty in understanding one another. Verstegan thinks that the English language should be as independent from its neighbors as they are from it:

Doubtlesse yf our selues pleased to vse the treasurie of our own toung, wee should as litle need to borrow woords, from any language, extrauagant from ours, as any such borroweth from vs: our toung in it self beeing sufficient and copious enough, without this dayly borrowing from somany as take scorne to borrow any from vs.[10]

Rather than borrow and be in debt to others, Verstegan suggests that English writers revive our discarded Teutonic words, simplifying their spelling when necessary to fit the current practice, and as an encouragement he presents a short dictionary of "our moste ancient English woords" together with their modern forms or the French words that have replaced them in current usage. Verstegan's list includes such words as *acyrred*, now replaced by the French-derived 'turned,' *aethrynne*, which he glosses as 'touche,' and *afgod*, 'idol.' A further sampling of words and their glosses gives *bead* 'prayer,' *binne* 'manger,' *bode* 'messenger,' *dome* 'judgment,' *dugud* 'vertue,' *ear* 'honor,' *frid* 'peace,' *gefengon* 'prisoner,' *heym* 'couerture,' *lareow* 'master,' *rode* 'crosse,' *scona* 'beautiful,' *theoda* 'nations,' *thorp* 'village,' and *wod* 'furious, mad,' a word that Verstegan notes is still in use in parts of England.

Verstegan elaborates on two interesting words, *freundine* and *mensca*, to show how useful their adoption might be. According to him, *freundine*, or *freundina* "a woman-friend, a shee freind," on the analogy of the German, would fill a semantic gap in the English language: "If one say that hee met or spake with a freind of his, it apeereth not whether it were with a man or a woman, where as we might in our language aswel distinguish the masculyne from the feminyne, as others in other languages do." And *mensca*, or *menesca* (plural, *menscan*), would be a suitable replacement for the generic, indefinite pronoun *man* which, according to Verstegan, has been all but ousted by the masculine reference of the word. Apparently unaware of his own use of generic *man*, Verstegan writes that *mensca* would mean

a humaine creature in general, to wit, either man woman or chyld.... It is a woord of necessarie vse as for example, a man beholding some lyuing thing a farr of in the feild, not wel decerning what it is, wil say it is either a man or a beast, now it may be a woman or a chyld, and so not a man, and therefore hee should speak more properly in saying it either a *mensce* or a *beast*. [pp. 219-28]

In addition to revivals and provincialisms, English could be expanded by compounding its native elements. Verstegan does not actually suggest this as a method of increasing the word stock of the language—although other Saxonists use it regularly—but he is aware that it is a primary word-building process for English, and that compounds allow English to express just as much as can be done in any other language:

> Our ancient language consisted moste at the first of woords of monosillable, each hauing his own proper signification, as by instinct of God and nature they first were receaued and vnderstood, but heerof grew this benefit, that by apt ioyning together of two or three of these woords of one sillable, new woords of more diuersitie of sence and signification were stil made and composed, according as the vse of them for the more ful and perfect expressing of the composers meanings did requyre. By which meanes it grew vnto that copiousness and perfection, that diuers beeing very wel learned in other toungs, haue much admyred this, when they haue not bin able to fynde any one vsuall woord in any language, for the which they could not giue the lyke in this, in the same very true nature and sense. [pp. 189-90]

Saxonism played an important role in Renaissance translations of the Bible into English. It has always been the Saxonist position that native English vocabulary is easier to understand and more suitable for the education of the masses than imported terminology, the meaning of which is only apparent to scholars of the classical and romance languages. Protestant translators, trying to make the Bible available to the general population, often sought to make their language as clear as possible by using plain words. Sometimes their zeal for plainness led them to stylistic excesses equal to the ones they sought to replace. The *Authorized*, or *King James Version* of 1611 charts a middle course between the sometimes obscure classical diction of the Papists and the equally awkward nativizing of the Puritans. In the preface, called *The Translator to the Reader*, generally credited to Miles Smith, the philosophy of translation is explained:

> Wee haue on the one side auoided the scrupulositie of the Puritanes, who leaue the olde Ecclesiasticall words, and betake them to other, as when they put *washing* for *Baptisme*, and *Congregation* in stead of *Church*: as also on the other side we haue shunned the obscuritie of the Papists, in their *Azimes, Tunkile, Rational, Holocausts, Praepuce, Pasche*, and a number of such like, whereof their late Translation is full, and that of purpose to darken the sence, that since

they must needs translate the Bible, yet by the language thereof, it may bee kept from being vnderstood.[11]

William Tyndale's translation of the *New Testament*, published in Worms in 1526, shows a Puritan avoidance of aureate diction and a taste for archaic and provincial English expressions. A.C. Partridge calls Tyndale's translation "the first to endeavour to capture the spirit of the Aramaic behind the Greek, in the narrative, lyrical and expository resources of his own tongue."[12] For the traditional *church, priest, grace, confession, penance,* and *charity* Tyndale substitutes *congregation, senior, favour, knowledge* (that is, 'acknowledgment of sin'), *repentance,* and *love,* only two of which, *knowledge* and *love,* qualify as Saxonisms. In his *Old Testament* translations, done in the 1530s, his native style is perhaps clearer. Partridge notes Tyndale's use of the words *bruterar* 'murmurer,' prophesier,' *daysmen* 'judges,' *earynge* 'ploughing,' *feldedevels* 'satyrs,' *gronynges, hanfasted* 'betrothed,' *hoorhed* 'grey-haired person,' *loweth* 'low-lying country,' *mesellynge* 'drizzle,' *overthwarte* 'perverse,' *strypes* 'wounds,' *tote-hill* 'watch-tower,' *tyllman* 'farmer,' and *welth* 'happiness' (p. 55). But despite the presence of some Saxonisms, French-derived *bruterar* and *mesellynge* (from the OF word meaning 'leper,' cf. MnE *measel*) and *strypes*, which comes from the Dutch, show that Tyndale was not so much concerned with purifying the English language as he was with writing a text that was free of the difficult Greek and Latin terminology of previous translations. In his attempt to make the Bible more accessible to the average English Christian, Tyndale simplified or nativized his diction without purging it of borrowings.[13]

John Cheke, on the other hand, who had been Regius Professor of Greek and Public Orator at Cambridge, as well as Secretary of State to Edward VI and, occasionally, tutor to the young Elizabeth, took a clear stand on the role of Saxon vocabulary in Biblical translation and in the language generally. Cheke may have been reacting in part to an edict issued by Bishop Gardiner in 1542 that sought to introduce more untranslated Latin into the Bible on the grounds that some terms lost force or meaning when they were translated.[14] But in a letter to Thomas Hoby in 1557 Cheke makes it clear that his main concern is with language, not dogma:

I am of this opinion that our own tung shold be written cleane and pure, vnmixt

and vnmangeled with borrowing of other tunges, wherein if we take not heed bi
tijm, euer borowing and neuer payeng, she shall be fain to keep her house as
bankrupt. For then doth our tung naturallie and praisablie vtter her meaning,
when she bouroweth no conterfeitness of other tunges to attire her self withall,
but vseth plainlie her own with such shift, as nature craft, experiens, and
folowing of other excellent doth lead her vnto: and if she want at ani tijm (as being
vnperfight she must), yet let her borow with suche bashfulnes, that it mai appear
that, if either the mould of our own tung could serue us to fascion a woord of our
own, or if the old denisoned wordes could content and ease this neede, we wold
not boldly venture of vnknowen wordes. [*Elizabethan Essays* 1:357-58n]

A comparison of Cheke's translation of Matthew (ca. 1550) with
that of Tyndale as well as with the *Geneva Bible* (1560) and the
Authorized Version (1611) shows that, while Cheke does not
entirely eschew Latinate and Romance vocabulary, he does in
many places substitute one of "the old denisoned wordes" or create
a new one according to "the mould of our own tung." For example,
he uses *stock* (or *degree*) in place of *generacion; achess* in place of
feuer; and *wiseards* in place of the traditional *Wisemen*. Obvious
imports are Englished by Cheke: *publicans* are *tollers, proselytes*
are *freschmen, Centurions* are *hunderders. Lunatike* becomes
moond, and *superscription* is rendered *onwriting.* Christian
technical terms are also Englished by Cheke: *crucified* is translated as *crossed, regeneration* as *gainbirth, resurrection* as
vprising or *gainrising,* and *apostle* as *frosent* (that is, 'sent
from'). Cheke translates *repent* using the native alternative,
forthink, and he turns *justified* into *quitt* and *pieces of siluer* into
silverlinges. Cheke uses *bewrai* 'make known,' and *grootes* instead of *pence. Hired servants* become *hiindes,* but *steward,* a
word dating back to Old English, is replaced in Cheke's translation
by the French *bailie,* and *pearls,* a Middle English word, is replaced by *margarites,* which derives ultimately from Latin but
occurs in Old English.

Cheke employs a number of Saxon-like self-explaining compounds where the other Bibles use phrases. He writes *menfishers*
for *fishers of men; bloudground* for *field of blood; oliues hil* for
the mount of olives; other spirited (or *deuelled*) for *possessed with
devils; helimp* for *child of hell; ye smalfaithd* for *ye of litle faith;*
and *sculplace* for *the place of dead men's skulles.* In addition,
Cheke partially nativizes *generacions of vipers* to *offspring of
vipers.* His *Elders* are now *aldermen,* and his *parables* are *bi-
wordes.* Where the *Geneva Bible* writes *the poore receiue the*

Gospel Cheke has *the beggars be gospeld.* Similarly *carried away into Babylon* is for Cheke *outpeopling...to Babylon;* and *loke not sowre* is *be not lowring.* For Sir John Cheke the *crown of thornes* contains simple native *thistles.*

Archaism and Saxonism are also found in the Renaissance outside of poetry and Biblical translation. One of the earliest English treatises on Logic, Ralph Lever's *The Arte of Reason, Rightly Termed, Witcraft* (1573) employs a technical vocabulary that is largely of native origin. Lever, Canon of Durham and tutor to the first Earl of Essex, had been exiled for religious reasons during the reign of Queen Mary and returned to England when Elizabeth ascended the throne. He wrote on canon law and other subjects as well as on logic. It is not clear to what extent his religion influenced his linguistic philosophy, but Lever is an avowed Saxonist who opposes the use of "straunge and inckhorne termes." He extolls the virtues of English monosyllables and their role in the expansion of the English vocabulary: "As for deuising of newe termes, and compounding of wordes, our tongue hath a speciall grace, wherein it excelleth many other, & is comparable with the best."[15] Lever felt that because he was teaching the art of logic for the first time in English, he should devise a suitable terminology. According to him, an Englishman knowing no Latin or Greek will readily understand a word like *backset*, a compound of two familiar monosyllables, while *predicate* will mean nothing to him at all. Furthermore, the use of native English vocabulary will be beneficial for the language: "Vnderstandable termes, compounded of true & auncient english words, do rather maintain and continue the antiquitie of our mother tongue: then they, that with inckhorne termes doe chaunge and corrupt the same, making a mingle mangle of their natiue speeche " (p. vi*).

Lever believes that new words should be created only when they are needed, and not when old ones already exist. He promises that his own compounds will be self-explaining, but he also takes care to provide a glossary for his book to aid those whose knowledge of English etymology is insufficient for them to sort out such words as *backset.* Lever's vocabulary is not entirely Saxon. He uses French derivations as well as native English terms, and though he does shy away from formal Latin terminology, his nontechnical vocabulary does not stress the native element. Even in his technical discussions Lever employs an occasional romance *substance* or *contrary*, and he often couples an imported term with a native one to facilitate comprehension, as in *his contrarie gainset*. We have no idea how Lever's work was received, but we may hazard a guess that his Saxon prose did not facilitate the acquisition of what was already a complex if not murky subject. A definition such as the following should cause the average reader several trips to the glossary: "Wordes which cannot be coupled and ioyned together in a true & perfect yeasay, are either differing wordes, or gainsettes" (p. 53).

Lever employs the Anglo-Saxon base *wit* in the term he uses to replace *logic: witcraft*. His use of this word antedates the earliest citation in the *Oxford English Dictionary* by thirty years. Lever may well have created this word and others not cited in the *OED*. Only one citation from Lever occurs in the *Dictionary: speech-craft*, defined as "knowledge or science of speech."

Lever also uses *wit* to produce *vnwittie* 'foolish, careless,' and *witnesses* 'authorities (human and nonhuman).' In fact, most of Lever's newly created terms are compounds, although only a few of them, for example *lykesounding words* 'homonyms,' and *like-meaning woordes* 'synonyms,' are clearly self-explaining. Other words based by Lever on the root *like* are *lykelyer* 'that which is more,' and its opposite, *vnlykelyer* 'that which is less,' as well as *aslyke* 'that which is equal to.' *Set* gives Lever *foreset* 'subject,' *backsette* 'predicate,' and *gaynset* 'opposite, contrary.' *Say* is Lever's most productive base. It does not appear unbound as a technical noun, although the *OED* cites *say* 'saying, proverb,' as contemporary with Lever, but it readily forms compounds in his work. *Saying* and *shewsay* both occur for *sentence;* and we also find *endsay* 'conclusion,' *foresay* 'premise,' *ifsay* 'conditional proposition,' *naysay* (also *denying term*) 'negation,' *yeasay* 'affirmation,' *parting shewsaye* 'disjunctive sentence,' and *saywhat* 'definition.'

The prefix *in-* is used in the words *inbeer* and *indweller*, Lever's equivalents of *accidens* (see *OED, inbeing* 'inherence') and *inholder* 'subject' (see below, Fairfax's use of the term to mean 'tenant'). *Mark* forms *yeamarke* 'all, some,' and its opposite, *naymarke* 'none, some not,' and *commers* are of three kinds: *forecommers* 'predictions, evidence of what will occur,' *aftercommers*, "remembrances and monumentes of that which hath bene," and *with-commers* 'evidence of what is presently occurring' (none of these words appears in the *OED*, but the *Dictionary* does note the strong combining power of *comer: newcomer, farcomer, night-comer, chance comer, incomer, nextcomer*).

Worke, Lever's term for 'effect,' combines to form the term *workman* (sometimes replaced by *doer*) 'agent' (the *OED* cites the term as referring only to human agents; Lever uses it to refer both to animate and inanimate causes). *Thing* is found in *forethings* 'precedents,' and *selfe thing* or *sole thing* 'individuum.' *Over-showe* is used for the technical *superficies* 'length and breadth without thickness;' *playnmeaning wordes* are those 'free from ambiguity,' replacing the Latin *univoca; storehouse* is used to refer to any general category which can be divided into a number of *roomes* 'subdivisions;' and *yokefellowes*, or *respecting termes*, are used for the Latin *relata, relatiua. Kynde* is used by Lever as the equivalent of *genus*, and *kinred* or *kindred* as the equivalent of *species*.

A number of Lever's words are calques of Latin logic terms. *Having* is used for *habitus* 'condition, quality,' and *finding (out)* appears for *invention. Privatio* is realized by Lever as *want of natural power; terminus* becomes *bounder; generatio* is *begetting;* and *coniugata denominatiua*, literally 'derived from a spouse,' is Englished as *ofsprings*. The *material cause* becomes the *matter* or *stuff; figura* is *ranke;* and question words are *demanders*. Of Lever's nontechnical vocabulary, two terms are striking. He uses the old form *wight* 'man, creature' to refer to animals, and his use of *whatsicallit* in the phrase, "Words that signifie all things without distinction, as a thyng, a matter, a whatsicallit,' antedates the earliest *OED* citation for such a word (*OED sv what-d'ye-call-'em*) by sixty-five years.

In his important study *Early Modern English* (1976), Charles Barber identifies two seventeenth century writers as Saxonists, Francis White and John Hare. However White, who was Bishop of Ely and wrote primarily on questions of religious doctrine, actually sees linguistic borrowing in English as useful and necessary for the improvement of the language. In *A Replie to Iesuit Fishers Answere to Certain Questions Propounded by His Most Gratious Majestie King James* (London, 1624), White tells his readers:

Nothing could more increase good literature, and polish barbarous Languages, than the often comparing of one Language with another, and the refining and inlarging of that which is rude, and ouer-narrow and sparing, out of Tongues more ample and elegant. Experience teacheth this in Great Britaine, whose deficient and rude natiue Language, by meanes of all sorts of Translations, is made most polite and copious. [p. 382]

John Hare, on the other hand, used Saxonism to foster his rabid hatred of the French. In his pamphlet, "St. Edward's Ghost, or Anti-Normanism; Being a Pathetical Complaint and Motion, in Behalf of Our English Nation, against Her Grand, yet Neglected Grievance, Normanism" (1647), Hare refers to England as a conquered nation which too eagerly applauds "Normanism and Francism, which the desert of our sins hath inflicted on us." He asserts that England is really a Teutonic nation, not derived "from the conquered relicks of ruined Troy," and reminds us that it was a Teutonic people that conquered France long before the Romans made their appearance in that part of the world. Hare proclaims the purity of English Teutonic blood, reminding his readers that the Conqueror was "but a Norman bastard," and assuring them that Saint Edward, the Confessor, was the last rightful English king.

Everywhere they look, according to Hare, the English are reminded of their captivity, particularly in the areas of law and language: "If we survey our language, we there meet with so much tincture of Normanism, that some have esteemed it for a dialect of the Gallick." In order to remedy the situation, Hare proposes a four-point plan. First he requires that William be stripped of the title "the Conqueror." He next wants all English monarchs to derive their lineage from St. Edward. Thirdly, Norman laws are to be abolished and replaced with Edward's laws, written in English *or* in Latin. And lastly, Hare would rid English of its French (though not its Latin) vocabulary. He asks,

that our language be cleared of the Norman and French invasion upon it, and depravation of it, by purging it of all words and terms of that descent, supplying it from the old Saxon and the learned tongues, and otherwise correcting it, whereby it may be advanced to the quality of an honourable and sufficient language, than which there is scarce a greater point in a nation's honour and happiness.[16]

Hare's Saxonism is a tempered one. He is not against borrowing so much as he is against anything French. He makes no effort to avoid nativized French words in his own writing, and it is not clear how he would handle the problem of words whose origin could be traced either to French or Latin. And finally, Hare makes no attempt actually to revive archaic or provincial Saxon words.

NATHANIEL FAIRFAX

In 1674 Nathaniel Fairfax, a clergyman, Baconian scientist, and physician, published a metaphysical study called *A Treatise of the Bulk and Selvedge of the World*, in which he used native English words to replace terms of foreign origin. Fairfax's prose is even denser at times than that of Lever, as the following example may indicate: "If...the Fryes of Wrigglers and swarms of Quicklings or Insects, peep out of their Graves and Dungeons, they must wait upon the Sun to bring about those beams of his that make the Spring; whence they may have their Prison doors unlockt, their fetters taken off, and be tickled into such a laughing briskness, and judged up into such a smirkish liveliness, as may last as long as the Summers warmth holds on to cocker them, and the days heat to frigge and chafe them."[17] In his *forespeech*, or preface, Fairfax explains his nativist style, discounting fancy and fashionable borrowings and praising the plainness, bluntness, and strength of an unmixed English:

As for the way of wording it, I know aforehand, 'tis not trim enough for these Gay days of ours; but dressing is none of my business. When I look at things, I can afford to overlook words, and I had rather speak home than fair, nor do I care how blunt it be, so it be strong.... There is one thing which I may be blam'd for by many; and that is a kind of shiness all along of those borrowed words & gaynesses, that Englishmen have pickt and cull'd from other Tongues, under the name of Choyce words and Sparkling sayings.... Thinking with my self, how I an English man would write a Book in English tongue, I made it now and than a little of my care, to bring in so many words of that speech, that the Book might thence be call'd English, without mis-calling it. And indeed however our smoother tongued Neighbours may put in a claim for those bewitcheries of speech that flow from Gloss and Chimingness; yet I verily believe that there is no tongue under heaven, that goes beyond our English for speaking manly strong and full. And if words be more to teach than tickle, as I reckon they are, our Mother tongue will get as much by speaking fit and after kind, as it can loose by faring rough and taking up the tongue to utter, and more than any else can gain, by kembing better and running glibber. [pp. B5^v-B6^r]

Fairfax acknowledges that all languages that derive from "the great *Speechbreak* at *Babel*" are blended ones, and he admits using "outlandish" words together with native English ones, "as thinking it unmeet to force my *words* upon another," but his aim is to use "hail and dear English" and to avoid "Cant words or terms of art." Fairfax, like many of the Saxonists, admires the language of the peasants and the working classes, in which he finds the antiquity of pure English preserved, and he remarks that "even the slighted and of-cast words in the mouths of Handy-crafts-men and Earth-tillers" are better to use than Latin. He advises his readers,

either to fetch back some of our own words, that have been justled out in wrong that worse from elsewhere might be hoisted in, or else to call in from the fields and waters, shops and work-housen, from the inbred stock of more homely women and less filching Thorps-men, that well-fraught world of words that answers works, by which all Learners are taught to do, and not to make a Clatter; And perhaps, if we slip this tide, we shall never come again at such a nicking one. [B7ʳ-B7ᵛ]

According to Fairfax, native words are closer to their referents than borrowings can ever be, for the latter are "as far off sometimes from the things they speak, as they are from us to whom they are spoken." Fairfax urges the resurrection of native English words, whether borrowed from the peasants who have preserved them for us or recreated on the analogy of native forms, for we can never really use imported words as they were used in their own lands. He says that we "may either find better words among our own Yeomanry...or at least coin fitter for new ones in a likewiseness to the old, than can be lent us from that Tongue wherein we know not how the Folks talkt in the Country, nor do any body else or ever shall do." Fairfax feels that such Saxonism could influence others to borrow our own words, reversing the balance of trade and canceling the slur "that *English-men* can do by their own Hands, what they can't speak in their own Tongues" (pp. B7ᵛ-B8ᵛ).

Fairfax uses more than four times as many Saxonisms as Ralph Lever does. His meanings are often unclear, even in their contexts, and unlike Lever, Fairfax provides no glossary for the edification of his readers. *The Bulk and Selvedge of the World* (that is, 'the mass or size, and horizon or limit, of the world') was read for the *OED*, and the *Dictionary* often cites Fairfax as the sole illustration of a word, marking the form as rare and obsolete. Seldom does the *OED* consider a Fairfax term a nonce word, although it would appear that many of his words qualify for such designation. In a number of cases Fairfax's is the earliest use cited, with no further occurrences until the nineteenth century, and in still other cases Fairfax uses words that are common enough native terms whose history goes back to Anglo-Saxon and which still occur in modern English.

Much of the Saxon flavor of Fairfax's writing derives from his use of monosyllables in contexts where we expect more Latinate diction, as in his persistent use of *bow* for *curvature* when speaking of the *bow of the earth*. Fairfax also uses terms that have a provincial ring, for example *coaks* 'simpleton,' *doaks* 'dimples, indentations,' *firk* 'hasten, urge on,' *fry* 'offspring,' *knack* 'contrivance,' *thwackt* 'clapped together,' and *yerk* 'jerk, strike.' Prefixed forms also abound in his writing. We find *a coming, a making,* and *a pieces,* as well as sixteen or more words beginning with the verbal prefix *be-,* including *becalm'd, bedewings, bedightings* 'affectations,' *bedim, befann'd, behove, beset, besmearing, beswoln, bewedding,* and *bewhispers.* Negative forms begin with Saxon *un-* rather than Latin *in-: unsay* 'deny,' *unsproutful* 'infertile,' *unbeholden* 'independent,' *uncouthness* 'illogicality, mystery,' and *unbeclogg'd* 'free-flowing.'

Saxon suffixes are also favored by Fairfax. Final *-en* produces third person, plural *biggen* 'grow;' participial *bounden, crowden, lucken, shotten;* and plural *workhousen.* Adjectival *-som(e)* gives us *cleavesome* 'partable, divisible,' *lightsom* 'luminescent, light in weight,' *flowsom* 'fluid,' and *throwfaresom* 'penetrable;' while *-less* provides *cleaveless* 'indivisible,' and *bodiless* 'immaterial.' The diminutives *-ling* and *-kin* are active in Fairfax's vocabulary, accounting for *scantling* 'measurement,' *shaplings* 'small forms, embryos,' *onwardling* 'a small portion or length of time,' *middlekin* 'medium,' and *somewhatkin,* the equivalent of Lever's *whatsicallit.*

Clearly the most productive Saxon morphological form for Fairfax is the nominalizing *-ness.* There are about fifty words that use this suffix, including *allfillingness, everywayness* 'immensity,' *formerness, latterness, herenesses, therenesses, moreness* 'plurality,' *piercelessness* 'impenetrability,' *soonerness, suchness* '?essence,' *thingsomeness* 'reality,' *thinkfulness* 'ability to think,' *wastfulness* 'desert, empty area,' and *whereness* 'ubeity.'

Compounds form the bulk of Fairfax's Saxon vocabulary. Most of these contain two morphological bases, although three-element compounds also occur: *half-thwart-line* 'radius, semidiameter (of the earth),' and *self-cut-throat* 'self-destroying, undercutting.' Of the two element kind we find, among others, *dead-doing* 'killing, causing death,' *fierdhalf* 'one fourth,' *holdfast* 'support, belief,' *outlanders* 'foreigners,' *puddering pole* 'pole to poke things with,' *same-kidneyed* 'similar,' *speechbreak* 'disruption of language,' *steamscope* 'atmosphere,' and *watchwright* 'watchmaker.'

In discussing the earth's measurement Fairfax uses *mete* 'to measure,' and its derivatives *metesom* 'measurable,' *meteing* 'dimension,' and *metwand* 'measuring stick.' A *meteing* may be one of three kinds, described as *little*, *middlekin*, or *mickle*, and they may even be referred to as *measures*, although as the following passage demonstrates, one does not have to go far in Fairfax's prose before meeting a Saxonism:

A *natural body is made up of Physical points, made up of Mathematical measures*. That is, 'tis not made of Mathematical points, but made of those things that are made of nothing but Mathematical points. A slie kind of body indeed, that is Mathematical at secondhand, or linsey Physical woolsey Mathematical. [pp. 106-07]

The following list contains words apparently created or used in a new sense by Fairfax; words for which Fairfax is the only *OED* citation; and words for which Fairfax is the sole citation for a particular sense. Also included are words for which Fairfax is the earliest or the major citation, and words, marked with an asterisk, which are not found in the *OED*. The list is not exhaustive; its purpose is to illustrate Fairfax's word-making rather than to provide a complete catalogue of his usage.

abiding Duration
allfillingness* Pervasiveness
alwayness Everlastingness
awarings of sense Perceptions
bear Elasticity, as of a spring
belongers Elements
betiders Indicators
bitlings Pieces, fragments
body-haunter* Spirit
bodyhood The quality of having a body
brack Atom
by-running Passing, going by
cantling Section, piece, part
charmwise In magical manner
cleaveless Indivisible
cleavesome Divisible
close Unity, oneness
dirtying Blasphemy
earlyerness Quality of being prior, or more early

evenliness Evenness, suitability
everbeing Eternal
everbeingness Eternal nature
everywayness Quality of stretching in every direction
everywhereness Ubiquity
fierdhalf One fourth
fleshward Towards or in relation to humanity
floudings Flood
flowsom Fluid, liquid
fondling Child, offspring (rather than the *OED* sense 'found child')
formerness Anteriority
fulfilledness* Quality of being fulfilled, fulfillment
ghost To inspirit (without *OED* sense 'haunt;' simply to endow with spirit)
gossipred Affinity
growthsom Fertile
half-thwart-line* Radius, semidiameter (of the earth)
hereness Fact or condition of being here, or present
hoghen moghen* ?Large (possibly related to *hugger mugger*, but apparently not in its sense 'secret, clandestine'): "Such a hoghen moghen Leviathan."
latterness Condition of being subsequent
leasting Atom, indivisible point
lifesomeness Liveliness
loadstoneships* Magnetisms
mayness* Possibility
meddle Mix (this sense apparently not common in mid and later 17th century)
metesom Measurable
middlekin* Medium (*EDD* has the word only in the sense 'tolerable')
minglement Mixture
moreness Plurality
nestwright Builder of nests
nicebrattling* Fairfax's meaning not clear: "A nicebrattling out of *reality*" (See *OED*, *sv brattle* 'to produce harsh sounds').
off-scourings Refuse; that which is scoured off
onefoldness Unity
onwardling A small portion or length of time
outstretchedness Extension
partable Divisible
pend Tendency, inclination, leaning
piercelessness Impenetrability
puddering pole A pole to poke with (*OED sv pudder* 'to poke')
raughty Raw, damp
rightning Put or set straight
roblet To lead astray (from *roblet* 'a goblin leading people astray in the dark')
roomthy Pertaining to space as opposed to time
roomthiness Existence or extent in space
roomster Occupant of space
round-dealing-wise Plainly, honestly
runlong Course (labeled by *OED* as a nonce word)

ruthfulness Compassion

self-cut-throat* Self-destroying, undercutting

shacking ?Covering up; "Those rayes of other atoms that are shacking all over the worlds wasts" (*OED* suggests 'to run at shack,' *shack* being grain fallen from the ear and available for feed, after harvest).

shortestness Minimal length

shaplings Small forms, embryos

shreadlings Minute, indivisible pieces

soonerness* Quality of being sooner

speechbreak* Disruption of speech or language: "The great speechbreak at Babel."

spratkin Small creature

spreadingness Extent

sprightness Sprightliness

springsomness Energy, elasticity

spungholes* Nooks (*OED sv spung* 'to rob')

steamscope* Atmosphere

stowsom Having position in space

stowsomness Location (*OED* labels this a nonce word)

stretchling A minute quantity of space

sturt Sudden impulse

sundership* Divisibility (*OED sv sunderness, sunderment*)

thereness Quality of being there

thingsomeness Reality

thinkfulness Ability to think

throwfaresom Penetrable

thwacker A thumping lie

timeishness Temporality

timesome Temporal, finite, located in time

twinship Identity

twin-trangham* An odd or intricate device (*OED sv trangam*)

unbeginningly Endlessly, eternal

unbeholden Independent

unmeetsomeness Immeasurability

utmostness Extremeness

wastfulness The state of being waste or void

watchwright Watchmaker

whereness Position, location

worldhood State or condition as a world

2. SAXONISM IN THE NEOCLASSICAL AND ROMANTIC PERIODS

In the eighteenth century, interest in Saxonism subsided as a reaction to Renaissance archaism set in. Some writers, however, still paid lip service to it. Samuel Johnson, for example, recommends in the Preface to his *Dictionary of the English Language* (London, 1755) that the Teutonic nature of English be preserved:

Our language, for almost a century, has, by the concurrence of many causes, been gradually departing from its original *Teutonick* character, and deviating towards a *Gallick* structure and phraseology, from which it ought to be our endeavour to recal it, by making our ancient volumes the ground-work of stile, admitting among the additions of later times, only such as may supply real deficiencies, such as are readily adopted by the genius of our tongue, and incorporate easily with our native idioms. [p. C1ʳ]

Yet Johnson was no Saxonist. His own prose is often pointed to as an example of excessive Latinism. The most "ancient volume" that he was willing to accept as a stylistic model was the work of Sir Philip Sidney. And Johnson's notions of linguistic borrowing are at best somewhat vague. He seems to feel that the French language made inroads into English not so much as a result of the Norman Conquest but because of the English presence on the Continent, for he says, "Of many words it is difficult to say whether they were immediately received from the *Latin* or the *French*, since at the time when we had dominions in *France*, we had *Latin* services in our churches" (p. A4ᵛ).

Satirist Archibald Campbell took Johnson to task for his use of borrowed terms and inkhornisms. Referring to Dr. Johnson as *Lexiphanes*, Campbell sees the very existence of English threatened by the influence of the great lexicographer. The question for Campbell is

Whether we shall continue to write and speak the language transmitted down to us by our ancestors... or whether we shall adopt, I will not say a new language, but a barbarous jargon, attempted to be imposed upon us, by a few Schoolmasters and Pedants... who think they have done a fine thing when they have tack'd an English termination to a Latin verb.[18]

But despite this indictment of Johnson, Campbell is not a Saxonist; he never even mentions the Germanic roots of English.

Despite the overall waning of interest in Saxonism in the eighteenth century, there were occasional appeals for the revival of old words. Writing to the *Gentleman's Magazine* in May, 1735, a correspondent suggests that since poetry makes liberal use of the terms and ideas of science, philosophic writing might benefit from the adoption of poetic ornamentation, which includes archaism: "Tho' the common Forms of our *Language* may here be too scanty for our *Ideas*, yet since nothing adds more to the *Majesty* of *Poetry* than a Deviation from the common Modes of Speaking, that Defect may be abundantly supply'd by a *Revival* of *antiquated* Words, which are confess'd to give a *venerable* Air to *Poetical* Descriptions" (5:252), and the author of "Fog's Journal" in the August issue of the same review regrets that the vocabulary of Chaucer and Spenser has been neglected by modern writers (5:466).

Discussing the translation of LeBlond's *The Military Engineer* in the *Critical Review* in 1759, it is suggested that, although French is the undisputed language of the art of war, we should try to introduce English, though not necessarily Saxon, technical terms when possible: "Why, for example, should we be so complaisant to the French, as to use their terms of *carcasse, cavalier, chamade, chausse-trappe, biovac* [bivouac], *chevaux de frise, abbattement, enfilade, feu-razant, manoeuvre*, and *coup de main;* when we can say, *fire-ball, mount, parley, crow's-foot, blocking-guard, turn-spikes, tree-felling, flanking-fire, grazing-fire, operation,* and *bold stroke?*" (8:178), although in the body of the review the writer reverts to the traditional French terminology.

Generally speaking, the use of obsolete terms was discouraged. In the *Critical Review*'s notice of Lewis's English version of the *Thebaid* of Statius, the translator is faulted for such obsolete words as *astounded, erst, 'gan, ween,* and *whilome:* "Our language has in vain been refined from impurities and enlarged by improvement, if we reject the present mode of expression, and go back for our words to the days of Chaucer and of Gower.... Old words can only please a reader who takes delight in turning over the leaves of a glossary" (23 [1767] :365). In his *Philosophy of Rhetoric* (London, 1776), George Campbell classes the use of obsolete words under barbarism. To Campbell antique words are as strange to the ear as the garb of our forefathers is to the eye; they "have no more title than foreign words, to be introduced at present" (1:410). Campbell rejects both those ancient words which are

completely obscure to the modern reader, for example *cleped,
erst, hight, uneath,* and *whilom,* and those words that are still
intelligible but, to his mind, are seldom used. Only critics and
antiquarians can still understand such words as *anon, behest,
erewhile, fantasy, peradventure, selfsame, tribulation,* and
whenas. As we can see, a number of eighteenth century writers,
including Samuel Johnson, declared the death of some words
prematurely.

Campbell does admit archaisms in poetry, where they may be
useful in treating antique subject matter or even required by the
laws of versification, and he also allows them in burlesque writing,
where the laws of decorum are customarily overthrown. But
Campbell finds new words, especially those borrowed from the
French, to be even more barbaric and dangerous to the language
than old ones, and he concludes by advising his readers to take a
middle course in diction, citing Pope's "Essay on Criticism":

> In *Words,* as *Fashions,* the same Rule will hold;
> Alike Fantastick, if *too New* or *Old.* [2:333-34]

The fate of Saxonism in the eighteenth century may be summed
up in a remark by novelist William Godwin: "It is probably of little
consequence whether the idiom of the English language... be Gal-
lic or Teutonic, whether it come from the East or the West."[19]

Noah Webster, the American dictionary-maker, bridged the gap
between the seventeenth and nineteenth century Saxonists. Webster saw English as a composite language, hierarchic in structure.
Its Saxon substratum, which was preserved in the language of the
yeomanry, represented for Webster the unimproved language
suitable for "the purposes of an agricultural people," past and
present, while the Graeco-Roman superstructure added by the
learned classes was "the language of a polite and improved nation."[20] Webster admired the peasantry and felt that farmers — at
least the American ones—had preserved "the primitive idiom,"
and that their usage should form the basis of the national standard.
The notion that the common people were the true guardians of the
language, a notion that influenced Romantic and later nineteenth
century attitudes toward language, caused Webster to recommend
that sermons and "other discourses designed for general use"
should not be composed in the elevated style, but should contain as
many Saxon words as possible.

Lindley Murray, an American who moved to England after amassing a fortune during the Revolutionary War and wrote one of the most influential school grammars of the nineteenth century, also warns against the overuse of borrowings: "Foreign and learned words, unless where necessity requires them, should never be admitted into our composition." Murray admits that Latin words can sometimes give elevation and dignity to style, but he adds "in general, a plain, native style, is more intelligible to all readers; and, by a proper management of words, it can be made as strong and expressive as this Latinised English, or any foreign idiom."[21]

In proposing an American linguistic standard, Webster favored the speech of his native New England, whose noble peasant stock preserved, at least for Webster, the purest English: "Their idiom is purely Saxon or English; and in a vast number of instances, they have adhered to the true phrases, where people, who despise their plain manners, have run into error." Webster claimed that New Englanders spoke better than the British:

They [New Englanders] say, if a person is not in health, he is *sick*. The modern English laugh at them, because the English say a man is *ill*; and confine sick to express the idea of a nausea in the stomach. The English are wrong, and the New England people use the word in its true sense. . . . Ill is a contraction of *evil*; and denotes a moral disorder. Its application to bodily complaints is a modern practice, and its meaning figurative. So that whatever improprieties may have crept into their practice of speaking, they actually preserve more of the genuine idiom of the English tongue, than many of the modern fine speakers who set up for standards. [*Dissertations*, p. 389]

According to Webster, corruption in language was caused not by the careless or decaying speech of the masses but by the efforts of the educated elite who actually defiled the tongue they sought to improve:

Custom among a whole people erects an impregnable bulwark against the assaults of innovation; and we are indebted to popular usage for the preservation of many English idioms, which writers and critics, from an affectation of refinement, have most injudiciously attempted to banish. It is a curious fact. . . that the principal corruptions of our language, within the last five hundred years, are the work, not of the vulgar, as is commonly supposed, but of authors and writers, pretending to purify and refine the language.[22]

While not referring specifically to questions of Saxonism, William Wordsworth, in his Preface to *Lyrical Ballads* (1802), argued that the vocabulary of the common people, or the language that people really use, was most appropriate for poetic diction. Later nineteenth century writers elaborated on this idea, and some of them came closer to a Saxonist line. For example, in an essay in the *Edinburgh Review* in 1830, Thomas B. Macaulay commends John Bunyan's "pure old Saxon" English:

The vocabulary is the vocabulary of the common people.... We have observed several pages which do not contain a single word of more than two syllables.... There is no book in our literature on which we would so readily stake the fame of the old unpolluted English language, no book which shows so well how rich that language is in its own proper wealth, and how little it has been improved by all that it has borrowed.[23]

There were nineteenth century antisaxonists as well. Thomas DeQuincey, writing on the English language in 1839, regarded Anglo-Saxon as a language with a vocabulary of only six to eight hundred words, "most of which express some idea in close relation to the state of war." DeQuincey saw the older elements of English as being of limited use, mainly for the expression of "simple narration, and a pathos resting upon artless circumstances, — elementary feelings, — homely and household affections." But what he called the "Latin moiety" of English is indispensable for any grand, complex, elaborate, or meditative feeling.[24]

In 1844 Samuel K. Hoshour, clergyman, Professor of Languages, and first president of Northwest Christian (now Butler) University, attempted to revive inkhornism. In his book, *Letters to Esq. Pedant in the East, by Lorenzo Altisonant, an Emigrant to the West*, Hoshour produced such words as *algidity* 'coldness,' *funambulist* 'rope dancer,' *geoponics* 'farming,' *proficuous* 'advantageous,' and *cynarctomachy* 'a fight between a dog and a bear.' Hoshour believed that students would learn difficult words more easily if they encountered them in such prose passages as the following:

In my precedaneous communications, I conducted you to the termination of my primal day's profluence. Soon after my vespertine repast of that day, I intimated to the caterer for human and belluine entities, that in consequence of feeling superlatively elumbated, I had a great prurience of early couchee, and that he should indigitate to me the dormitory in which I might enjoy somniferous quietude.[25]

Hoshour intended his work as an introduction to Latin and Greek terms in English, but in his glossary he silently includes archaic and provincial terms, or Saxonisms, as well. Actually Hoshour is more an archaist than a Saxonist, for a number of the terms that he revives are Middle English borrowings from French, and unlike the other Saxonists Hoshour does not create his own new terms. Few of his Saxonisms are compounds: *clod-pate* 'awkward fellow,' *cotquean* 'one who meddles with women's affairs,' *wantwit* 'simpleton,' and *wealsman* 'a mean politician.' Most of his Saxonisms are labeled as archaic, obsolete, or dialectal by the *OED*. They include such words as *anent, betide, bosky* 'woody,' *bushet* 'a wood,' *brank* 'buckwheat,' *chuff* 'clown,' *cleg* 'horsefly,' *cole* 'cabbage,' *doodle* 'simpleton,' *duds* 'old clothes,' *eam* 'uncle,' *ethel* 'noble,' *fausen* 'an eel,' *frith* 'woods,' *fussock* 'a large woman,' *hafter* 'wrangler,' *heppen* 'neat, decent,' *lab* 'a great talker,' *lemen* 'sweetheart,' *leod* 'the people,' *lever* 'rather,' *sess* 'tax, assessment,' *sickerness* 'safety,' *skeg* 'wild plum,' *sarse* 'sift out,' *sweven* 'dream,' *wain* 'wagon,' *wample* 'disposed to vomit,' *welkin* 'sky,' *went* 'path,' and *yaud* 'horse.' Some of Hoshour's definitions differ from those of the *OED*. For example, he explains *amble* as 'walk carefully,' while the closest *OED* sense seems to be 'walk in an easy motion'; and the *OED* does not define *bye* as 'dwelling,' or *dern* as 'sorrowful,' as Hoshour does.

The poet Walt Whitman, eager to enlarge the vocabulary of English by almost any means, cautions against the unnecessary use of foreign words. Writing in *Life Illustrated* in 1856 Whitman proposes a list of some 110 words, most of them French but a few of them Italian, for which he sees a need in English. In asking for their adoption, Whitman reminds his readers not to use any foreign word if the audience being addressed might not understand it. He introduces his list by saying, "Some of these are tip-top words, much needed in English—all have been more or less used in affected writing, but not more than one or two, if any, have yet been admitted to the homes of the common people" (1:185). Whitman's list includes words that are quite familiar now, for example, *aplomb, brochure, bourgeois, cabaret, facade, genre, morgue* (which Whitman translates as 'dead-house'), *penchant, resume,* and *suite*. Other words on the list are familiar to many English speakers, although they are still recognized as French. These include *allons, attache, bon jour, bon soir, bon mot, en route, faubourg, insouciance, jeu d'esprit, roue,* and *trottoir.* Whitman's suggestion of *portfuille* [sic] is made in apparent violation of his own criterion that a word must fill a gap, for *portfolio* appears in English as early as 1722, and three words that Whitman marks as especially desirable have proved remarkably unsuccessful, two of them, *abrege* 'abridgment' and *auditoire* 'place of the audience in a public building' (this is Whitman's gloss) no doubt because the language already contained cognates for them and the third, *attrister* 'sadden' perhaps because it did not lend itself to nativization according to English verb patterns: even Whitman's democratic language would have trouble embracing *attristed* and *attristing*. Other French words that Whitman recommends have also failed to make their way to the heart of our language, among them *accoucheur* 'man-midwife,' *bienseance* 'propriety,' *embonpoint* 'fat, pursy,' *feuilliton* 'little leaf,' and *voltigeur* 'vaulter, soldier in the light cavalry' (this last word is occasionally used in nineteenth century English, particularly as a French military term).

WILLIAM BARNES

A number of nineteenth century authors actually used Saxonisms seriously in their work. The romantics and later poets used archaisms, pseudo-archaisms, and dialectal terms to flavor their writing, and Sir Walter Scott, Thomas Carlyle, and William Morris used Saxonisms even more extensively as an integral part of their diction. William Barnes, a teacher and clergyman, combined poetry and philology, writing several volumes of verse in his native Dorset dialect. These proved popular, and a collection of his poems was edited by Thomas Hardy, another writer with a great interest in dialect. Barnes also wrote in prose, publishing, among other things, two grammars and a logic text in which he used native English terms, many of his own devising, to replace technical and nontechnical French, Latin, and Greek borrowings. While he apparently did not use his own Saxonisms or his Dorsetshire dialect in conversation, Barnes did make an effort to couch his sermons in simple, direct, non-Latin English.

In "Compounds in the English Language" (1832), Barnes takes his first major stand against linguistic borrowing, lamenting the fact that "the English are a great nation; and as an Englishman, I am sorry that we have not a language of our own." Barnes argues that Latin may be elegant in sound to English ears, but it is not elegant in shape. He praises Addison and Byron for their non-

Latinate style, and condemns writers like Johnson for encouraging useless borrowings: "Are poets killed so often that we want the word vaticide?"[26]

Barnes finds that some borrowings unnecessarily duplicate words already present in the language, for example *annual* and *yearly, subterranean* and *underground, corporal* and *bodily, decapitate* and *behead*. In addition, he feels that new words are borrowed from Latin and Greek rather than being formulated on English models largely because of the bias of scholars. They are simply ignorant of the principles of Gothic word formation and consider the native element of English to be rude and useless. Barnes suggests the formation of new English words on native models. Using the formative *-lorn*, for example, he produces *waylorn* 'having lost one's way,' and *glorylorn* 'having lost one's glory,' as well as *reasonlorn, childlorn, mastlorn*, and *hopelorn. Fare* 'to go,' is used to form *landfaring* 'going by land,' and *airfaring* 'going by balloon.' *Dom* 'the jurisdiction of,' gives *chiefdom, mayordom, commissionerdom*, and *masterdom* (Barnes is silent on the fact that the roots of some of these words are not Saxon); while *-rich* yields *shiprich* 'having much shipping,' as well as *landrich, minerich, fruitrich, spicerich*, and *wordrich*. He would distinguish the adjectival forms *iron* and *ironen:* an *iron tool* is one with which iron is worked, while an *ironen tool* is one made of iron. Barnes also suggests *silken, floweren, strawen, metallen*, and *papern* on the model of *golden* 'made of gold,' and *linen* 'made of lin, or flax.'

In 1842 Barnes published his *Elements of English Grammar*, a book designed "to keep up the purity of the Saxon English language" while explaining to students the principles of English etymology and presenting a scientific syntax of the language. Barnes used this grammar in his own schoolteaching, but it was not widely adopted by others. In the *Philological Grammar* (1854), an attempt at Universal Grammar which compared English with sixty other tongues, Barnes's Saxon style becomes prominent: he substitutes the term *breath-sounds* for *vowels; clippings* take the place of *consonants; breath-sound language* replaces *speaking;* and *type language* is used for *printing*. Barnes renames the traditional Latin case categories, too, *nominative* becoming *the mainspeech case, possessive* becoming *the what's case, accusative* being replaced by *the whereunto case, locative, the where case,* and *dative, the what-to case* (Barnes posits a total of twelve different cases for English).

Early England and the Saxon-English (1869), a historical account of Anglo-Saxon England, was also written in a Saxonized style, and in the chapter on the English language Barnes states his Saxonist manifesto:

English has become a more mongrel speech by the needless inbringing of words from Latin, Greek, and French, instead of words which might have been found in its old form, or in the speech of landfolk over all England, or might have been formed from its own roots and stems, as wanting words have been formed in German and other purer tongues.

Because of this constant borrowing, which Barnes blames on the anti-German prejudice of the barely competent Latin and Greek scholars at the English universities, the common people are denied participation in the culture of England, which becomes the exclusive property of an elite group of classicists:

Thence English has become so much harder to learn, that, in its foreign-worded fulness, it is a speech only for the more learned, and foreign to unschooled men, so that the sermon and the book are half lost to their minds: whereas in Tuscany and in the west of Ireland, or in Wales, the speech of the upper ranks is that of the cottage, and the well-worded book of the higher mind needs no list of hard words to open its meaning to the lower.[27]

This radical sociolinguistic philosophy, that a common dialect should unite English peasants, workers, and aristocrats, is carried even further in the *Outline of English Speech-Craft* (London, 1878), in which Barnes, showing his complete commitment to Saxonism, presents examples of what the vocabulary of such a dialect might be. In this book, a treatise on English grammar, Barnes attempts, as he tells us in his *fore-say,* or 'preface,' "one small trial, weak though it may be, towards the upholding of our own strong old Anglo-Saxon speech, and the ready teaching of it to purely English minds by their own tongue" (p.iii). Barnes feels that using native vocabulary for *lore-words,* or 'scientific terms,' will facilitate comprehension, make difficult material more readily available to the masses, and religion more accessible to them: "The Latinish and Greekish wording is a hindrance to the teaching of the homely poor, or at least the landfolk. It is not clear to them, and some of them say of a clergyman that his Latinised preaching is too high for them, and seldom seek the church" (p.88).

Barnes warns that unless his Saxonist approach is imitated by

others, "Ere long, the English youth will want an outline of the
Greek and Latin tongues ere he can understand his own speech"
(p.iv). He develops a technical vocabulary for grammar, or *speech-craft*, in which a proposition is a *thought-wording*, its subject a
speech-thing, and its predicate a *time-taking*. The sounds of Eng-
lish consist of such things as *breath-pennings* 'stops,' *half-pen-
nings* 'spirants,' and *free-breathings* 'vowels.' These form
clusters of *breath-sounds* 'syllables,' and these in turn form words
that are *one-sounded* 'monosyllabic,' *tway-sounded* 'disyllabic,' or
many-sounded 'polysyllabic.' The *word-strain*, or 'accent,' falls
on a particular *breath-sound*, and the word itself may be a *thing-
name* 'noun,' a *name-token* 'pronoun,' a *mark-word* 'adjective,' or
a *time-word* 'verb.' Nouns may be *matterly* 'concrete,' or *unmat-
terly* 'abstract,' and pronouns may be of the *stronger* (or *carl*) *sex*,
the *weaker* (or *quean*) *sex*, or they may be *unsexly* 'neuter.' Under
the heading of *speech-trimming* 'syntax,' Barnes discusses the
possible cases of nouns, including the *of-spoken thing case* 'nominative,' the *end case* 'accusative,' the *to-spoken thing case* 'voca-
tive,' the *source case* 'dative,' the *stead case* 'locative,' the *tool
case* 'instrumental,' and the *allfree case* 'absolute.'

In *An Outline of Rede-Craft (Logic) with English Wording*
(London, 1880), Barnes presents a nativized technical vocabulary
for logic (he is apparently unaware of the work done earlier by
Ralph Lever in the sixteenth century). Discussing *shapes*, or
'*figurae*,' Barnes gives an example of a *three-step thought-putting*
'syllogism':

> Every two-horned beast—is cud-chewsome,
> Every two-horned beast—is grass-eatsome,
> Some grass-eatsome beast—is cud-chewsome. [p.26]

Barnes is a purist as well as a language planner, and he objects to
miswordings, or 'solecisms.' In the *Outline of English Speech-
Craft* he insists that Latin borrowings that are retained in English
should represent legitimate Latin forms, and he complains when
"one man writes of something which *necessitates* another, though
Latin itself has no *necessito* to back 'necessitate' " (pp. 36-37).
Barnes is also literal-minded about English etymology, arguing
that a *twin* refers to two people, and *twins* must therefore refer to
four. Barnes would revise the order of some English compounds so
that they are headed by *case words* 'prepositions,' calling for

downfalls, incomings, offcuttings, outgoings, upflarings, off-casts, and *outlockings* to replace *falls-down, comings-in, cuttings-off, goings-out, flare-ups, cast-offs,* and *lock-outs.* Hybrid borrowings, or *mongrel words* such as *sub-warden, ex-king, pre-paid,* and *bimonthly* are in his mind "a sore blemish to our English, as they seem to show a scantiness of words which would be a shame to our minds" (p. 43). Barnes suggests as alternatives to these *rodless* or *crownless king, forepaid* (ignoring its mongrelized French base, *pay*), and *fortnightly.*

In addition to his insistence on logic, Barnes wants English to sound more pleasant, and to this end he would revise the *somely,* or 'plural' forms of nouns ending in *-st* to *-stes* or *-sten,* as in *fist, fistes, fisten:* "What in the world of speech can be harsher than fists, lists, nests?... It is unhappy that the old ending in *-en,* which is yet the main one in West Friesic, should have given way to the hissing *s*" (p. 8). Some of his Saxon substitutions similarly improve the sound pattern of English by reducing the number of sibilants and harsh and unpleasant consonant clusters: "*Past,* with the hissing *s* with *t,* is less sound-good than *after;* and *aqueduct,* with *ct,* is less well-sounding than *waterlode;* nor is *cataract* softer than *waterfall*" (pp. 39-40).

Saxonization must be conducted carefully according to Barnes, and the creation of new words must follow correct English models. He finds, for example, that *scoundreldom* is an incorrect use of *-dom* and actually means "the right of scoundrels as ruling or judging." *Scoundrelhood* would be the appropriate noun (p. 58). Barnes also objects to the nominal suffix *-ism,* revealing as he does so a touch of anti-Semitism: "For *-ism,* taken in names bestowed with very slight praise, we may take *-ishness;* as, *Hebraism, Hebrewishness*" (p. 65).

Barnes concludes his work on *speech-craft* with a comment on the quality of language, emphasizing the need for clarity in sound and sense, and arguing that the best languages do not borrow but are enlarged by the building of new words from native elements. Like the Saxonists before him, Barnes's prose is often difficult to follow:

The goodness of a speech should be sought in its clearness to the hearing and mind, clearness of its breath-sounds, and clearness of meaning in its words; in its fulness of words for all the things and time-takings which come, with all their sundrinesses, under the minds of men of the speech, in their common life; in sound-sweetness to the ear, and glibness to the tongue. As to fulness, the speech of men who know thoroughly the making of its words may be fullened from its own roots and stems, quite as far as has been fullened Greek or German, so that they would seldom feel a stronger want of a foreign word than was felt by those men who, having the words *rail* and *way*, made the word *railway* instead of calling it *chemin de fer*, or, going to the Latin, *via ferrea*, or than Englishmen felt with *steam* and *boat*, to go to the Greeks for the name of the *steamboat*, for which Greek had no name at all.

According to Barnes, borrowing does not necessarily increase the size of the English word stock, for imports tend to drive out native words, often when they should not: "The fulness of English has not risen at the rate of the inbringing of words from other tongues, since many new words have only put out as many old ones, as:— immediately, anon (no saving of time here)" (p. 86).

Some of Barnes's suggestions for Englishing vocabulary are reasonable: *quicken* may often replace *accelerate; forbear* is certainly more familiar now than *absist;* and *booklore* may sometimes mean 'literature.' Others are not so well thought out: *going over again and again* is an unwieldy substitute for *iterative,* and *wanting something of its kind* seems an ineffective replacement for *defective.* Barnes is also inconsistent in some of his suggestions. He would have *deprave* Saxonized to *forshrew* or *forwarp,* while *depraved* is realized by *wicked. Forfray* is used by Barnes to mean both 'abrade' and 'deter.' And *forloosen* replaces *absolve,* while *forloosening* is to mean 'analysis.' *Apocope* is translated into *endlopping,* but *aphaeresis* becomes *foredocking.*

Barnes uses several principles to produce his new Saxon vocabulary. Some borrowings are simply translated or paraphrased: for example *inbringing* for *importation* and *last but two* for *antepenultimate.* In other cases English words are re-semanticized, or given new meanings to accord with borrowed terms: *hank* 'coil,' is now to mean 'appendix,' and *odd-shaped* is to be used instead of *anomalous.* But what Barnes likes to do best is revive archaic or provincial words, make up new words with a dialectal or antique flavor (generally by using the affixes *for-, fore-,* and *-en*), and form compounds using native English monosyllables.

In his verse Barnes, who was known as the Dorset poet and who published a grammar and word-list of the Dorset dialect, used a great number of provincial expressions. In his prose he uses only a few: *brangle* 'altercation,' *doughty* 'active,' *flaundering* or *glavering* 'adulation,' *halesome* 'salubrious,' *sprack* 'active,' and *up-*

cleam, or *cleam up* 'agglutinate.' Barnes uses dialect words to form compounds. From *dunt* 'strike, drive out,' and *dill* 'assuage,' he forms *pain-dunting* and *pain-dilling* as possible replacements for *anodyne. Spell,* obsolete in the sense of 'message' but still active in dialect compounds, provides Barnes with *wire-spell* 'telegram,' and *spell-wire* 'telegraph.' *Wort* 'plant,' is the basis for *wortlore* 'botany,' and *welkin* 'sky, heavens,' leads Barnes to *welkin-fire* 'meteor,' and *welkin-air* 'atmosphere.'

In one case Barnes re-Saxonizes, changing *alone* to *all-an* or *all-one* in order to make its etymology more transparent, but he does not notice the inconsistency between his treatment of this word and his creation of *forloned* 'desolate.' Barnes would revive native English disease names, for example *hipwork* 'sciatica,' *hrop-werc* 'colic,' *sid-adl* 'pleurisy,' and *wildfire* 'erysipelas.' *Twy* 'two,' allows Barnes to form *twy-breathed* or *twy-aired* 'amphibious,' and *twy-meaning* or *twy-sided* 'ambiguous.' *Wone* 'to live,' and *stead* 'place,' produce *wonestead* 'domicile.' And *weeking* (from *Viking*) suggests itself to Barnes as a replacement for *pirate.*

The following list of words that are not already noted above contains many, but not all of the neo-Saxon vocabulary to be found in Barnes's prose work. Starred words do not appear in the *OED.* Perhaps because of personal difficulties between Barnes and Francis J. Furnivall, the mercurial head of the Philological Society and a moving force behind the *OED,* neither the work on *speech-craft* nor that on *rede-craft* was read for the *Dictionary,* although there are some citations from Barnes's poetic endeavors in it. Words marked with a + are to be found in the *OED* but in a sense different from that given by Barnes. And words marked with a # are labeled by the *Dictionary* as obsolete, archaic, or dialectal.

afterkin+ Posterity
all heal# Panacea
atsetting* Antithesis
beholdingness# Indebtedness
bendsome Flexible (the sole *OED* citation is that of Barnes)
bestopping* Punctuation
bidding mood* Imperative mood
book-lore+ Literature
brangle, # **brangling**# Altercation
carry over+ Metaphor
cellar-thane* Butler (*OED sv cellarman*)

child-teams* Generations
daysman# Arbitrator
deemsterhood* Criticism
ereold* Antique
fair wording* Euphemism
faith-heat* Enthusiasm
faithlaw* Religion
fallsome* Deciduous
folkdom* Democracy
folkland* Country
folk-leader,* **folk's-ringleader*** Demagogue
folk's-reder* (*folk* +*reden* 'to judge') Demagogue
folkswording* Idiom
folkwain* Omnibus
foraying* Affirmation
forcarve+ Amputate
fore-eking* Prefix
fore-elder# (also, **kin-elder***) Ancestor
foreold* Antique
foretake (also, **foreween**) Anticipate
forfreen* Absolve
forlikening* Allegory
fornaughten* Annihilate
fornaysome* Negative
forshapening* Accidence (*OED sv forshape* 'metamorphose')
forsoak* Absorb
forstonen* Petrify
forstonening* Fossil
forwaste# Depopulate
frowards Perverse
gin Machine
giving case* Dative case
hairbane* Depilatory
henchman Attendant
high-deedy Magnificent
house-twin* Semi-detached house
hue# Species
kind Genus
kin-stem* (also, **forekin-stem***) Pedigree
leafen + To foliate (*OED* has only adj form, *gold-leafen*)
letter-shuffling* Anagram
loan-meed* (also, **loan-pay,*** **money-rent***) Interest
loosensome* Laxative
lore-speech* Lecture (*OED sv lorespell* 'sermon, discourse')
makingness* Faculty
manqualm# Epidemic
matter-quickness* (also, **fire ghost***) Electricity
new bewording* Paraphrase

nipperlings* (also **tonglings**) Forceps
offspring case* Genitive case
offturning* Apostrophe
offwriting* (also, **wording-share***) Paragraph
onquicken* Accelerate
outclearening* Exegetical
outeking* (also, **helping**) Auxiliary
(un)overfaresome* (In)transitive (*OED sv overfare* 'pass over, cross')
push-wainling* Perambulator
rank-fellow* (also, **rank-mate**) Coordinate
rede-craft* (also, **redelore***) Logic
rede-speech* Oration
rim Horizon (*OED* labels this use 'poetic')
sky-line (also, **sky-sill***) Horizon
soaksome* Bibulous
song-mocking* Parody
soundly* Phonetic
statespellman* Ambassador
sunder-speech* (also, **fortongueing,*** **folk-speech**) Dialect
teaching (also, **teachsome***) Didactic
thought-cullings* Aphorisms
threaden# Filaceous
thwartsome* Adversative
time+ Tense
tithe Decimate
to and fro verb+ Reciprocal verb
touting-sheet* (also, **touting-bill***) Circular
two-horned rede-ship* Dilemma
unfolk* Depopulate
unfrienden# Alienate
unfullening* Depletion
unmaking+ (also, **forloosening**) Analysis
updrawing* Contraction
warestore* Emporium
water-awe* Hydrophobia
waterlode* Aqueduct
weapon-stay(ing)* (also, **war-pause**) Armistice
white-hot (also, **heat-whitened**) Incandescent
word-book Dictionary
word-building* Etymology
wordling* Particle
worth-evenness* Equivalent
wrangling+ Argumentation
year-bookings* Annals
year-day+ Anniversary
year-dole* Annuity

While Barnes's dialect poetry was well-received by reviewers, his efforts at nativizing the English prose vocabulary were met with some skepticism. The *Saturday Review* simply notes a number of his suggestions, adding that if he does no more, Barnes may "deal a blow at some of the blunders and absurdities of modern English speech," while the *Athenaeum* is less hopeful, saying of Barnes's Saxon diction that "the words have a deterrent effect." The reviewer finds Barnes's words uncomfortably close to the comic language of the recently published *Alice in Wonderland*, though he adds that some readers "will have a kindly feeling for the chivalrous attempt which is made...to preserve the purity of our mother tongue." Archibald Ballantine, writing in *Longman's Magazine*, is less kind and objects to any sort of fanatical purism in language. Citing an example of Barnes's prose, Ballantine accuses him of "a want of literary sanity."[28]

Martin Farquhar Tupper

According to his entry in the *Dictionary of National Biography*, Martin Farquhar Tupper, author of poems, plays, essays, and novels, was the darling of the middle classes in the nineteenth century. His English, it is said, was more like German, and his name came to stand for commonplace and worthless verse. Be that as it may, Tupper did contribute in his own small way to the Saxonist movement by translating the poems of King Alfred, specifically his meters of Boethius, from Old English into modern verse that was heavily flavored with Anglo-Saxon vocabulary. The translations of *King Alfred's Poems* (London, 1850), undertaken for a jubilee edition of Alfred's works, were later included in Samuel Fox's edition and translation of Alfred's *Boethius*. Tupper says that in making his translation his intention was "to keep the still used words of our ancient Anglo-Saxon tongue wherever [I] could, and to throw aside all Latinized and other mixed forms of expression." Tupper claims to have rendered his verses "into such primitive English as that a Saxon may readily understand them," and he expresses the hope that some old words may be revived by his efforts: "What a pity it is that any of the fine old root-words of our tongue should have been forgotten.... We have of late years been throwing away, by the hundred, the stout old props of our strong north-country speech, and have substituted in their stead the sesquipedalia verba of Southern Europe. Nothing then can be more wholesome than to return for awhile to such good plain stuff as Alfred's stalwart Anglo-Saxon" (pp. 3-4).

In his translation of Alfred's poems, Tupper makes free use of Anglo-Saxon words, simply modernizing whenever possible. Such forms as *earl, earthlings, fastness, land-churl, mid earth, shieldmen, seastream, swart, thane, waxed, welkin,* and *word-hoard* render fairly faithfully Alfred's original, while *angel-land, house-herd, outlandish, quickened, thwarter,* and *wealdom* lend a Saxon air to the poetry. But Tupper does not confine himself to Saxonisms. Arguing that Latin words can be found in Old English, he feels free to use the Saxon-Latin compound *weird-ordain'd* for Alfred's *wyrd gescraf,* as well as such borrowed words as *despoil'd, fray, grant, mercy, peace, people, power, reign, royally, rule* (for Old English *rice*), *seize, verity,* and *vowed.* And, with the exception of a short five act play, *Alfred* (1858), an overrwrought account of the great king's battle with the Danish invaders in which characters with authentic sounding names speak a highly Latinized neo-Shakespearean verse, Tupper does not again venture into the Saxonist fray.

A SAXONIST TEXTBOOK

In the 1850s an American group identifying itself only as "a Literary Association" published a series of three textbooks for the instruction of young children in the fundamentals of English vocabulary. The first, *A Hand-book of Anglo-Saxon Root-words* (New York, 1853), consisted of a list of one thousand Anglo-Saxon root words felt to form the basis of every English speaker's core vocabulary, while the second, *A Hand-book of Anglo-Saxon Derivatives* (New York, 1854), demonstrated how these root words could form the basis of new words with the addition of prefixes and suffixes of native origin. The third volume in the series, *A Handbook of the Engrafted Words of the English Language* (New York, 1857), demonstrated the construction of Latin and Greek words to expand the basic English vocabulary of the first two handbooks. The *Hand-book of Anglo-Saxon Derivatives* begins with an address by one Dr. Wisdom on the excellence of the Saxon part of our language. Anglo-Saxon, according to the good Doctor, should be preferred to Latin or French in early education because the words of the home, the heart, and early life, the sensible and practical words, and the grammar of the language are all Anglo-Saxon in origin. Latin is too abstract for the young, and French is not suitable because "the French portion of our language is associated with wrong and oppression" (p. viii). Dr. Wisdom sees a new freedom for the mother tongue:

The time is at hand when the professor of the English language shall sit side by side with the doctors of Latin and Greek; but he shall do so on the condition of placing the old Anglo-Saxon above the classics, and making Alfred and Caedmon and Bede more honorable than Virgil and Homer. Gentlemen, our old mother-tongue has endured two captivities: one under the Norman-French, the other under the Latin and Greek. From the former, it was delivered under the reign of a king: from the latter, it is about to return under a president. [p. x]

Most of the five thousand Anglo-Saxon derivatives recommended in the *Hand-book* are still familiar terms. For example, the base word *home* produces *homes, homely, homelier, homeliness, homeward, homebound, homedwelling,* and *homesick*. It also produces *homelily,* a word cited by the *OED* as early as 1489 and as late as 1755, when it appeared in Samuel Johnson's *Dictionary;* by 1854 the word must have had an archaic or provincial ring to it. *Creeky, sandish,* and *shelfy* are also classed as obsolete or archaic by the *OED*, while *lanker* and *lankest,* the comparative and superlative of the adjective *lank,* and *lankiness,* its nominalization, are not found in the *Dictionary* at all. The Saxonist work of the Literary Association that produced these handbooks was undercut by the third volume in the series, the *Hand-book of the Engrafted Words of the English Language*, which stressed new adoptions from Latin and Greek but grudgingly admitted that "the practice of using French words and phrases in English speech, although in bad taste, has introduced many words into our language" (p. 28).

3. THE LATE NINETEENTH AND EARLY TWENTIETH CENTURIES

The late nineteenth and early twentieth centuries saw both the last major efforts of Saxonism in the work of Elias Molee and Charles Louis Dessoulavy, and the onset of a strong reaction against the Saxonist movement on the part of most students of the English language. While Dessoulavy, like William Barnes, simply advocated the replacement of borrowed terms with words of Germanic origin, Molee tried to create a new Saxon language, with reformed grammar, orthography, and lexicon, as a replacement for what he saw as a mongrelized, weak, and inefficient English tongue.

ELIAS MOLEE, SAXON LANGUAGE PLANNER

Elias Molee, an American writing in the late nineteenth century, was the most prolific and visionary of the Saxonists, attempting to devise an international "union" language to serve all Germanic nations. Molee called this tongue by a variety of names: *American Language, Germanic-English, Pure Saxon English, Nu English,* and *nu teutonish,* and just as he was unable to decide on a single name for his creation, Molee was unable to make up his mind which linguistic reforms to include in it. Among the many proposals Molee considered between 1888 and 1919 are the replacement of Arabic numerals with alphabetic letters; a system of phonetic spelling using a revised alphabet; a simplified spelling system retaining the standard alphabet; the replacement of all capital letters with lower case forms; and abbreviations for the commonest English words: for example, *e* for *the, n* for *and, t* for *to, z* for *as, v* for *of.* Molee urged the creation of morphological distinctions between plural and possessive nouns (*two handa* 'two hands,' *Godo haus* 'God's house'), between weak preterites and past participles (*he lovo* 'he loved,' *he has loven* 'he has loved'), and between gerunds (to be indicated by *-ing*) and participial adjectives and present participles (to be indicated by *-and*): *he is goand, the flyand bird, good hearing.* Molee proposed the introduction of an indefinite pronoun, *man* (from the German) and a common gender pronoun, *ir,* and he advocated both the abandonment of grammatical gender and the restoration of masculine and feminine nominal suffixes (*broi* 'brother,' *broa* 'sister;' *fadi* 'father,' *fada* 'mother'). But what underlies all of Molee's proposals is a radical Saxonism.

Molee sees in English a potential world language, but he warns that before global linguistic domination becomes possible English must achieve supremacy over itself. According to Molee, English must become "self-explaining, pure and homogeneous like the ancient Greek, Irish, modern German and Skandinavian."[29] English must not borrow from other languages but must develop itself from within. Like many Saxonists, Molee finds fault with French, one of the major polluters of English, for its double nominatives, double negatives, clumsy comparison of adjectives, bad spelling, lack of a neuter gender, nasal twang, and for being "very full of idiotic expressions where words mean something entirely different from what they appear to mean" (p. 20). Because the Normans were originally Scandinavians, Molee holds the Norwegians personally responsible for the French domination of the English language and for the fact that "the English speak...as a conquered people," and he suggests that the Norwegians can make amends by allowing us to borrow back Germanic vocabulary from them when necessary. English mixed with French, Latin, and Greek is a slave language for Molee, and as such it has no place in a democratically organized America: "English is not produced naturally by a free people, and it is hardly good enough for our free America, because it is too wasteful of mental energy and cannot be readily understood" (p. 50).

Molee echoes a common belief of Saxonists when, in urging that Americans not disregard the opportunity to reform their language, he claims that a nativized English will make knowledge and progress available to the common people, who are presently excluded from learning and science by the obscurity of the Greek and Latin technical vocabulary. For Molee America affords a unique opportunity to apply reason in the reformation of language and to free its inhabitants from bondage to the dictionary:

In England the poor are so poor that they cannot spend any time on language, and the rich are so rich that luxury or business overwhelms them. America has a composite population, where respect for English is less strong, and if we were wise enough here to take advantage of that fact, we have an opportunity now to put the world into the possession of the best language in existence, because it will have the light, experience and achievements of other languages to build upon. A language in which words and rules will be arranged in rows and beds, as plants in a garden, instead of growing up without order, as flowers on the wild prairie. [p. 112]

In support of his proposals, Molee cites the work of James Hadley, chemist, literary critic, and Professor of Greek at Yale. In his *Brief History of the English Language,* printed as an introduction to the 1864 edition of *Webster's American Dictionary of the English Language,* Hadley finds English as a language superior to French and German in terms of the freedom of word order, but he finds it inferior in its word-making abilities:

[English] no longer possesses the unlimited power of development from its own resources which we see in the Anglo-Saxon and in the modern German. If a new word is wanted, instead of producing it from elements already existing in English, we must often go to the Latin or the Greek, and find or fashion there something that will answer the purpose. By this process our language is placed in a dependent position, being reduced to supply its needs by constant borrowing. But it is a more serious disadvantage that in order to express our ideas we are obliged to translate them into dead languages. The expressiveness of the new term, that which fits it for its purpose, is hidden from those who are unacquainted with the classic tongues; that is, in many cases, from the great body of those who are to use it. To them it is a group of arbitrary symbols, and nothing more. The term thus loses its suggestiveness, and the language suffers greatly in its power of quickening and aiding thought. [Webster's *Dictionary,* 1873 ed. p. xxix]

Molee's major reform involves the replacement of foreign words in English with native ones, when they are available. But ironically, when native words do not exist Molee advocates borrowing from "the living German form of the Anglo-Saxon" rather than reviving obsolete Old English words (p. 163). He is, in short, a Germanist, not an antiquarian or a reviver of provincial terms. If German words are not available or are inappropriate, Molee recommends that words be borrowed from the Scandinavian languages. For example, *prayer,* of French derivation, must be replaced, but Molee thinks that German *Gebet* sounds too much like English *betting,* and he offers Scandinavian *bön* as the preferred form.

Molee sees one advantage of a homogeneous language to be "a freer flow of vivacity and cheerfulness.... The spirit moves easier in a self-developed tongue, as there is less fear, at least with many of the guests, to misplace accent and to misapply some foreign word" (p. 157). He prefers self-explaining native compounds because they aid thought and are more heroic, beautiful, and good. In foreign compounds, on the other hand, "there is no light, no love, no friendly accommodation to understanding and memory, no respect for the people, no patriotism."[30] Molee suggests that the Romanic peoples ought to create their own union language, and he envisions a league of Teutonic and Romanic speakers forming a strong bulwark against the threat of Pan-Slavism in Europe.

In *Pure Saxon English; or, Americans to the Front* (1890), Molee provides lists of recommended Saxon *forsilba* and *aftersilba* 'prefixes' and 'suffixes,' as well as Saxonized technical vocabularies for grammar, mathematics, botany, physiology, geography, and zoology, and a general collection of over 1,800 Saxon substitutions for common English words. Molee's Saxonisms are spelled phonetically, but here for convenience his *q* for [a] and inverted *i* for [i] have been silently rewritten as *a* and *i*.

Molee does not always replace borrowings with Saxonisms, although that is his intent. He sometimes translates unnecessarily, for example substituting *lafel* for *laughter* and *Nuenglander* for *Yankee*. *Grosson* is probably not much of an improvement on *grandson*, and *midi* is a questionable replacement for *center*. Although he refers to the work of William Barnes, Molee creates his own native vocabulary. He avoids archaisms and provincialisms, though he does include *sith* 'boil.' Many of Molee's Saxonisms are simply German words borrowed whole into English, for example *mut* for *courage*, *shön* for *beautiful*, and *kunstler* for *artist*. Others are Englished versions of German: *bekanti* 'acquaintance,' *bukstaf* 'letter' (Molee may have taken this form from Old English *bocstaef* or German *buchstab*), *entwepon* 'disarm,' and *foroldik* 'antiquate.' Molee relies heavily on what he feels to be self-explaining compounds: for example, *almight* 'omnipotence,' *autkreiword* 'exclamation,' *florkleid* 'carpet,' and *nirstep* 'approach.' And a good number of his words are compounds of native English elements, some, like *fudstor* 'grocery,' already in common use, others merely possible: *handtoken* 'signature,' *hikin* 'masculine gender,' *shikin* 'feminine gender,' *plantwul* 'cotton,' *sheepflesh* 'mutton,' *snikmurder* 'assassinate,' *speechlore* 'grammar,' *upgo* 'ascend,' *worldall* 'universe,' and *woundhealer* 'surgeon.'

The following list is a small but representative sample of Molee's lexicon:

adl Noble   **ahundred** Per cent

ar Honor
birdir Barber
brainspin Fantom
calfflesh Veal
deerflesh Venison
deerlore Zoology
deiik Mortal (from *dö* 'die')
deiikeit Mortality
dir Animal
dorf Village
doterman Son-in-law
earhealer Aurist
elder Senator
entblum Deflower
entfremdu Alienate
erin Remember
eyehealer Oculist
fangi Captive
fasister (also, mosister) Aunt
fershort Abbreviate
fi Cattle
findship Enmity
fishlore Icthyology
folgplan Program
folgweisik Fashionable
forthat Because
füg Join
ganfil Antipathy
gefolk Nation
gegenstand Grammatical object
gesenti Ambassador
geshikti History
gewördalist Lexicon
hart-hind Pericardium
hausli Domestic
hevenik (also, godik) Divine
hirbar Audible
holimaikel Sanctification
holion Altar
hun Cent
inbirthik Native
ingehav Viscera
inwei Consecrate
inwilik Consent

landrat Congress
lernling Apprentice
lipik Labial
lovsom Amiable
mitrat Conference
onlet Feign
ontrust Confidence
overgo Excel
overstep Exceed
postum Postage
ratslag Counsel, deliberate
redu Blush
richik Ample
rongu Err
shaimflek Blemish
shaivkneif Razor
shreibweir Telegraph
skuler Pupil
sloterer (also, fleshseler) Butcher
smokston Chimney
spraki Language
stablist Alphabet
sukdira Mammal
thrugang Alley
toothhealer Dentist
trekum Magnetism
tubelong Appertain
tugiv Concede
umsaiel Grammatical subject
umspikl Topic
unari Dishonor
unredlik Dishonest
wachsom Alert
wedbraik Adultery (Molee gives ferfols and
    ferderb as substitutes for *adulterate*)
wedum Marriage
weg Away, off
weiffather (also, manfather) Father-in-law
weisi Way, manner
whimisik Capricious
winkel Angle
wishfeineri Luxury
word-treasury Vocabulary
zins Monetary interest

CHARLES LOUIS DESSOULAVY

Charles Louis Dessoulavy, a translator of religious works from

Italian and German and a compiler of dictionaries of Maltese and Arabic, published the *Word-Book of the English Tongue* in 1917. The last of the major Saxonists, in his word-book Dessoulavy gives "Teutonic" equivalents for several thousand French and Latin loan words in English. Unlike Barnes and Molee, Dessoulavy is not himself an inventor of Saxonisms. Although he silently borrows the invented words of others, including a number from Barnes, Dessoulavy claims that all his words can be found in print in more or less the same sense within the past fifty years. He also suggests that new words may be formed at will "by tacking on to the English words the olden endings (-en, -ing, -ish, -ness, -hood, -ship, -dom, -ric, &c." (Dessoulavy is apparently unconscious of his use of the abbreviation for the Latin *et cetera*).[31]

Dessoulavy does not provide his readers with much in the way of explanation for his work, but it is clear that his motivation is anti-French rather than pro-German. In the *Foreword* to the *Word-Book* Dessoulavy states that "English folk...have been seeking to shake off the Norman yoke that lies so heavy on their speech.... There are many who feel not a little ashamed of the needless loan-words in which their speech is clothed." Dessoulavy thinks that borrowing is so ingrained a habit with us that "English is no English at all but sheer French," and he wants to do whatever he can to remedy the situation and restore the older unmixed language:

For liveliness and strength, manliness and fulness of meaning, the olden English Tongue were hard to beat. The thought-world, too, of those who think in the olden Saxon Tongue is utterly other from that of those who think in Norman French. It is, maybe, to their love of the Tongue of their Fathers that our singers owe much of their witchery.

In fact, as Dessoulavy sees it, a knowledge of French or Latin can only be an encumbrance to a speaker of English: it is difficult enough to find the best English word to suit an occasion, but "it is the more learned (owing to their better knowledge of the southern tongues) who are most often at a loss to find the true word after which they are seeking" (p.v).

A typical entry in Dessoulavy's word list shows a number of equivalents for a particular term. Thus while *diploma* can be replaced by *sheepskin* (labeled by the *OED* as U.S. usage), and *diplomat* gives way to *trimmer*, *diplomatic* may be realized by *crafty*, *deft*, *far-seeing*, *foxy*, *shrewd*, and *sly*, words which tell us more about Dessoulavy's opinion of diplomats than about the process of Saxonization. *Immerse* can be rewritten *bathe, dip, drench, dowse, drown, duck, flood, overflow, overwhelm, steep, swamp, bury, dive, sink;* and *immersed* becomes *beset, over head and ears, knee, &c. -deep. Water-drinker,* Dessoulavy's replacement for *teetotaller,* is also accompanied by an editorial comment: *those who drink water, think water.*

Like previous Saxonists, Dessoulavy relies on compounds for many of his loan-word replacements. He suggests *blackman* as well as the less polite *blacky, darky,* and *thick-lips* for the borrowed word, *Negro,* and he offers the dialectal *cheek-tooth, mill-tooth,* and *grinder* for *molar.* Dessoulavy revives a number of words labeled obsolete, archaic, or rare by the *OED*, including *bewield* 'govern,' *earth-tilth* 'agriculture,' and *fire-raising,* a Scottish legal term for 'arson.' Sometimes Dessoulavy uses a phrase as the equivalent of a single word. The result is usually awkward: for *alternate* he suggests both *see-saw* and *now one now t'other;* for *Renaissance* we are given *the Awakening* and *the New (Birth of) Learning.*

The following list is a very brief selection from Dessoulavy's work. Words that do not appear in the *OED* are starred, while those appearing in the *Dictionary* in a sense different from Dessoulavy's are marked with a +. Words borrowed from William Barnes have not been included.

(after)bite Remorse (*OED sv again-bite*)
arrow-headed (also, **wedge-shaped**) Cuneiform
axle (also, **axletree, shaft, spindle**) Axis
belly-god (also, **eat-all, greedy-gut(s), sweet lips**) Glutton
bethralled+ (also, **under one's foot**) Subject
bewield Govern (marked obsolete by *OED*)
beword+ Report
blind-gut (also, **blind-tharm**) Caecum
boo (also, **hoot**) Decry
bookcraft (also, **bookdom,*** **booklore**) Literature
bookery (also **book-hoard, book-house**) Library
bow-wow Onomatopoeic
brain-sick (also, **mad, moon-struck**) Demented
breach of wedlock* Adultery (*OED sv spouse-breach, -break*)
breeding (also, **teeming**) Pregnant
bring down Abate
burial ground (also, **God's acre, graveyard, lich-rest, bone-yard**) Cemetery
byspell (also, **byword, household word, saw, saying**) Proverb

clash (also, **slog**) Percussion
cranky[+] Abnormal
croaker Pessimist
day-bed Sofa (*OED* marks this obsolete)
dim (also, **fishy, left-handed, loose, misty, rambling, two-edged, unsettled, neither fish nor fowl nor red herring**) Ambiguous
eat one's heart out Repine
eating-house (also, **eating-room, chop-house**) Restaurant
foot-licker[+] (also, **body-guest**) Parasite
fore-read (also, **foreword, fore-say**) Preface
foster child (also, **fosterling**) Protege
fourth month April (the other months are similarly identified by number)
fowl-house Aviary
foxy Curious, diplomatic
gainsayer Adversary
glee-mote* (also, **sing-song**) Concert
goody-goody[+] (also, **mar-glee***) Puritan
gospeller Deacon
greenhorn Idiot
grit[+] Ability
haplihood* Possibility (*OED sv haply*)
hartshorn Ammonia
heart-burning (also, **lip-biting, thorn**) Annoyance
holed Porous
holt (also, **hurst**) Forest
horse-leech (also, **dog-leech**) Veterinary
hussif (also, **work-bag**) Reticule (marked obsolete by *OED*)
ingoing Entrance (marked rare by *OED*)
inwit Conscience (marked obsolete by *OED*)
kidnap Abduct
kingless[+] Democratic, republican
landsman (also, **townsman**) Compatriot (marked rare by *OED*)
lately (also, **whilere**) Recently
leak (also, **ooze**) Percolate (marked obsolete and dialectal by *OED*)
leech (also, **healer**) Physician (marked archaic by *OED*)
liverish Dyspeptic
loresmen Scholars
lung-sick Consumptive
manikin Puppet
midrif Diaphragm
misbirth Abortion (marked rare by *OED*)
nether[+] Sublunar
overdo Parody
prick (also, **seat**) Elect (marked obsolete by *OED*)
puffy Sententious (marked rare by *OED*)
reckon Add
reckoning Arithmetic
sawbones (also, **bone-setter, the knife***) Surgeon (marked slang by *OED*)

scratch-work Graffito
self-working (also, **penny-in-the-slot**) Automatic
shew-holiness* (also, **snivel**) Hypocrisy
singer (also, **rimer, scald**) Poet
song (also, **stave**) Poem
stem-tree* (also, **kin lore**) Genealogy
sweat-hole Pore
timber-wright* Carpenter
tit-bit Delicacy
tool Organ
twelve-monthly Annual
(between) two stools Dilemma
unbosom Confess
underyoke (also, **bring to heel**) Subject, v. (*OED* sole citation is from Wycliffe, 1382)
unlikeness+ Contrast
unsay Abjure
web (also, **weftage, woof**) Texture
wheelman Cyclist
whelp Puppy
whisk away Abduct
womanish+ Delicate
the yellows Jaundice (*OED* marks this as referring chiefly to horses and cattle)

4. REACTIONS TO NINETEENTH CENTURY SAXONISM

Many of those who took notice of the Saxonist movement of the nineteenth century were hopeful of its success. It was widely claimed by the Saxonists and their supporters that the native element of English was purer, stronger, and more emotional than the borrowed vocabulary, and even critics of Saxonism admitted its usefulness for poetry. Philosopher Herbert Spencer, in his *Philosophy of Style* (New York, 1873), praises Saxon English as being more "forcible" than Latin English. While Spencer recognizes the possibility that polysyllabic words may sometimes be stronger, or more emphatic, than their native monosyllabic counterparts, he finds that because the young child's vocabulary is almost wholly Saxon, the association between word and idea in Saxon English is reinforced: "The earliest learnt and oftenest used words, will, other things equal, call up images with less loss of time and energy than their later learnt synonyms." In addition to being more readily available, Saxon English is seen by Spencer as more economical: "If it be an advantage to express an idea in the smallest number of words, then will it be an advantage to express it in the smallest number of syllables" (p. 13).

Literary historian and editor Joseph Gostwick echoes Spencer's stylistic appraisal of Saxon English in his *English Grammar: Historical and Analytical* (London, 1878). Gostwick, like many writers on Saxonism, finds the native element of English to be more appropriate to poetry than to other modes of discourse: "Latin words, in poetry, cannot have the force of such pure English as was often written by Wordsworth" (p. 200). Gostwick even provides directions for those who would Saxonize their style: "If a student wishes to write English so that his words may be mostly Teutonic, he has little more to do than to take care about nouns, adjectives, and verbs; for the other words *must* be mainly Teutonic" (p. 180). Even Richard Grant White, critic, journalist and self-styled language purist, author of *Everyday English* (Boston, 1880), speaks warmly of the nineteenth century German effort to substitute native words for Latin and Greek borrowings in their scientific vocabulary and in the vocabulary of everyday speech. White feels that this move was beneficial for both the German language and the German national character, and he suggests that speakers of English might profit from the German example

(p. 471). And in *Words and Their Uses* (1870; 19th ed., Boston, 1891) White complains of our propensity for borrowing fancy words:

Petroleum means merely rock oil. In it the two corresponding Latin words, *petra* and *oleum*, are only put together; and we, most of us, use the compound without knowing what it means. Now, there is no good reason, or semblance of one, why we should use a pure Latin compound of four syllables to express that which is better expressed in an English one of two. The language is full of words compounded of two or more simple ones, and which are used without a thought of their being themselves other than simple words—*chestnut, walnut, acorn, household, husbandman, manhood, witchcraft, shepherd, sheriff, anon, alone, wheelwright, toward, forward,* and the like. The power to form such words is an element of wealth and strength in a language; and every word got up for the occasion out of the Latin or the Greek lexicon, when a possible English compound would serve the same purpose, is a standing but unjust reproach to the language—a false imputation of both weakness and inflexibility. The English *out-take* is much better than the Latin compound by which it has been supplanted—*except*. And why should we call our bank-side towns *riparian*? In dropping *wanhope* we have thrown away a word for which *despair* is not an equivalent; and the place of *truth-like*, or *true-seeming* would be poorly filled by the word which some very elegant people are seeking to foist upon us—*vraisemblable*. If those who have given us *petroleum* for *rock-oil* had had the making of our language in past times, our evergreens would have been called sempervirids. [pp. 215-16]

Lawyer and historian T. L. Kington Oliphant, in *The Sources of Standard English* (London, 1873), laments the loss of our old Teutonic words, blaming the incursion of foreign terms not, as was often customary, on Chaucer, but on the Franciscan friars of the thirteenth century. Kington Oliphant feels that "the only thing that could have kept up a purely Teutonic speech in England would have been some version of the Bible" (p. 221), but unfortunately Wycliffe used "un-Teutonic idioms" and the Reformation came too late to undo much of the damage. He praises Tyndale's Bible translation for keeping England steady to her old speech and guesses that had the Reformation not triumphed in England, "our mother tongue, thought unworthy to become the handmaid of religion, would have sunk (*exinanited*) into a Romance jargon, with few Teutonic words in it but pronouns, conjunctions, and such like" (p. 304).

Praising William Morris's "The Earthly Paradise" for "an almost purely Teutonic diction," Kington Oliphant urges every writer to revive "at least one long-neglected English word," and he himself uses *tongue* for *language* as well as *baleful, behoof, bespoke, brethren, churls, doughty deed, homespun* 'native,' *ken, kinsmanship* 'relationship,' *leechcraft, lore, maker* 'poet,' *sundry,* and *swinkers,* among others. He presents three sample sentences, all versions of the same text, to illustrate the differences between Teutonic English, the English of the period after William the Conqueror, and the Latinate English of the modern penny-a-liner:

I. Stung by the foe's twitting, our forefathers (bold wights!) drew nigh their trusty friends, and were heartily welcomed; taught by a former mishap, they began the fight on that spot, and showed themselves unaffrighted by threatening forebodings of woe.

II. Provoked by the enemy's abuse, our ancestors (brave creatures!) approached their faithful allies, and were nobly received; instructed by a previous misfortune, they commenced the battle in that place, and proved themselves undismayed by menacing predictions of misery.

III. Exacerbated by the antagonist's vituperation, our progenitors (audacious individuals!) approximated to their reliable auxiliaries, and were ovated with empressement; indoctrinated by a preliminary contretemps, they inaugurated hostilities in that locality, and demonstrated themselves as unintimidated by minatory vaticinations of catastrophe. [pp. 344-45]

In *The New English* (London, 1886), Kington Oliphant reiterates his support of Saxonism, praising the writing of Burns, Scott, Carlyle, and William Barnes. He is optimistic that the English of the future will more accurately reflect the English of the past: "If our English Makers set themselves earnestly to the task (they have already made a beginning), there is good hope that our grandchildren may freely use scores of Chaucer's words that we ourselves are driven to call obsolete." He blames the middle classes for "an amazing love of cumbrous Latin words, which have not long been in vogue" and the national educational system for its "lofty disdain for homespun English," and he feels that in replacing the Teutonic element of English with words borrowed from the French "we took brass for gold." Kington Oliphant notes that the French are not themselves borrowers of words, and he recommends a practical approach to Saxonism: a good writer "will never discard a Teutonic word without good reason; and if he cannot find one of these fit for his purpose, he will prefer a French or Latin word, naturalized before 1740, to any later comer." Yet despite this advice, Kington Oliphant fails to set a good example, speaking always of the *Lingua Anglica* instead of the *English language,*

and defining words by means of Latin rather than English synonyms in order, he claims, to avoid confusion.[32]

Responding to *The Sources of Standard English*, Herbert
Thurston, S.J., Catholic authority on false spiritualism and writer
on numerous religious subjects, takes Kington Oliphant to task for
blaming French loan words on the friars. Thurston feels that the
Protestants are as much, if not more, to blame: "We have to thank
the pedantry of the seventeenth century for all that is really
objectionable in Romance words, whereas those which belong to
an earlier period are for most purposes as valuable as the primitive
Teutonic."[33] According to Thurston, a Saxon revival might have
been appropriate when English began to reassert itself after the
Norman Conquest, when the old words still lived dimly in memory
or in the provinces. Now such words are utterly foreign to us, and
any appreciation of archaisms must be an acquired taste. He
rejects the "mysterious" notion of the Teutonic genius of our language, and he argues that a yearning for the old words is mis-
directed: "What was the word *maker* or *shaper* to the Anglo-
Saxon?...It conveyed no idea of sickly sentiment, of serenades
and moonlight, of long-hair and scented note-paper.... The old
Saxon word may really please us more than its modern rival, but it
is pure fancy; the fancied relish of home-made bread or home-made
ale, as compared with the equally wholesome productions of our
baker or our brewer" (pp. 362-65).

Thurston feels that archaism has a place in poetry, but if we
transfer old words from poetry to ordinary language they will lose
their special flavor. A mixed language such as English offers the
writer variety of expression, something which French, for example, lacks: "The French...have to write their tragedies in almost
identically the same language which they employ for the drama of
common life or for sober history" (p. 368). And referring to Kington Oliphant's examples of Saxon, Norman, and Latin style (see
above), Thurston finds the Saxon version to be as affected as the
Latinate one. The Anglo-Norman example, which Thurston sees
as "scarcely more than a caricature of English," at least stands as
proof that the best language is a mixed one (p. 373).

Another historian of the English language, J.M.D. Meiklejohn,
Professor of Education at the University of St. Andrews, regrets
the fact that the purest part of our language has now become
foreign to us: "Indeed, so strange have some of our own native

English words become to us, that sentences composed entirely of English words are hardly intelligible." Meiklejohn feels that native English is most strongly present in our spoken language: "It is the genuine English words that have life and movement; it is they that fly about in houses, in streets, and in markets; it is they that express with greatest force our truest and most usual sentiments—our inmost thoughts and our deepest feelings."[34] And Charles Mackay, poet, journalist, and language planner who favored restoring gender to English nouns and reforming English spelling, suggested in 1890 that authors might set an example "of restoring to daily use the words that were good enough for Wickliffe, Tindal, Chaucer," apparently unaware that many of these were of foreign origin.[35]

Poet, editor, and Professor of English at the University of Minnesota, Richard Burton, in "The Renascence in English" (1895), echoes the arguments of the nineteenth century Saxonists, praising the return to the simple and indigenous and the eschewing of the foreign in matters of language, and seeing Saxonisms as more than a temporary fad. Burton advocates evolution, not revolution, in language, "not the rooting up of what is firmly planted in the speech, but a reintroduction, a calling back of the germane, thereby ousting slowly, unviolently, what is less suitable." His program amounts to linguistic Darwinism: "It will be, and should be, a case of the survival of the fittest." Burton sees poetry as the primary vehicle for the Saxon revival, and he praises William Morris, whom he calls a "natural *trouvère*" [rather than a *maker* or *singer*] for his nativist tendencies. For Burton, Saxonism is not to be confused with other linguistic fads such as Euphuism or preciosity, which are marked by affectation. He finds no affectation but only naturalness in the return to the older forms of English, "a going back to what is simple, strong, direct, and vital to our speech instincts." However, like Kington Oliphant, Burton does not always employ the native vocabulary of the writers he praises. Besides calling Morris a *trouvère*, Burton's love of French frequently shines through in his writing. Of Saxonism he says, "Sometimes it shows in the literary regeneration of a word which for centuries has lain *perdu*." And he adds, "The very fact that our leading writers wish thus to turn back to native uses and things is, so far as it goes, proof of the race's health, of its solidarity and *esprit de corps*."[36]

Percy Bicknell, a librarian at the University of Illinois and a reviewer for the *Dial*, responded to Burton with an article entitled "The Retrogression in English" (1895). In his critique of Burton's evolutionary Saxonism Bicknell argues that the fittest forms of language have already survived and triumphed: "[Burton] looks for too great an enrichment of our speech through a return to native English words and turns of expression which have long ago demonstrated their inferiority to foreign importations, and perhaps even their uncouth and unmanageable nature, by allowing themselves to be crowded out of the language by substitutes of greater flexibility or euphony." Regarding Saxonism as a step backward and the Norman Conquest as a fortunate fall, Bicknell finds the purification of the German language an inappropriate model for English: "German, owing to its less fortunate history, has retained all its provincialisms, while English... has freed itself of the purely insular and local in its vocabulary and structure." He finds German unfit for the expression of technical information: "Vague and sometimes ridiculous are the scientific terms of the Teuton: *coal-stuff, sour-stuff, water-stuff* and *stifle-stuff*," and he warns against the linguistic inbreeding advocated by the English Saxonists. With irony Bicknell notes that the Saxonists cannot argue their case for native English without employing Latinate diction. He faults Burton for his gallicisms and for his failure to recognize Germanic words that have made their way into Latin and French. Burton, for example, cites *massacre* as a Latin-French replacement for the native English *blood-bath*, but Bicknell insists that the word, related to the German *Metzger* 'butcher,' originally came into Latin from a Germanic source.[37]

Lexicographer James Champlin Fernald is another critic of the Saxonists. In his *Expressive English* (New York, 1919), Fernald baldly states, "We have done better to borrow," and he praises the capacity of English to absorb foreign words: "Instead of painfully piling home-grown syllables upon each other or jamming words together under hydraulic pressure of thought, we may simply reach out and raid the universe of speech" (p. 77). Fernald notes the tendency of everything on earth, including language, to decay (though his examples show some misunderstanding of linguistic history or the process of language change): "The noble Hebrew has become the degenerate Yiddish, as spoken in the Jewish quarters of our cities.... [and] we see what wholly illiterate people can make of a language by the dialect of our Southern negroes" (pp. 238-42). Fernald has no use for decadent English whatever its presumed source: "The world has long since outgrown the Anglo-Saxon vocabulary. Those substantial old words give meaning in solid blocks, where modern thought needs fine discriminations. The advance of science, invention, and mechanism has brought in wholly new objects and relations for which we need words that the Old English stock can not supply" (p. 299). In *Historic English* (New York, 1921), Fernald adds that the mixture of French with Anglo-Saxon saved the English language from the dangers of inbreeding: "The language and the people were saved from that too intensive culture that breeds in and in, that makes a language and a people incapable of seeing beyond the horizon of their own civilization, and leads them to consider everything, however uncouth or monstrous, as good, beautiful, and sacred, so long as it is their very own" (p. 95).

Many writers found a need for both native and borrowed terms in English. William Mathews, holder of the Chair of Rhetoric and English Literature at the University of Chicago and author of *Words; Their Use and Abuse* (Chicago, 1877), accepts the native element of English but asserts that the use of Saxon alone would be a foolish economy: "The Saxon has nerve, tenseness and simplicity; it smacks of life and experience, and 'puts small and convenient handles to things,—handles that are easy to grasp'; but it has neither height nor breadth for every theme." Mathews finds Saxon suitable for simple narrative, elementary feelings, and homely and household affections, while grand passions, and meditative discourse "would languish or absolutely halt without aid from the Romanic part of the vocabulary." Like Herbert Spencer, Mathews finds that Saxon is the dialect of the nursery and therefore strongly associative. He advises his readers never to use a Romanic word when a Saxon one will do, and never to refrain from using one when Saxon will not do as well; in short, he says, "Do not over-Teutonize from any archaic pedantry" (pp. 170-81).

Textbook writer Jessie M. Anderson also accepts both native terms and borrowed ones in *A Study of English Words* (New York, 1897), although she too differentiates them into what has become a stereotypical classification: "The short, simple, everyday Saxon words are like farmers and shoemakers and carpenters, without whom a country could not get on at all; while the Latin words—longer, more elaborate, and more scholarly—are like what we call professional men, who go more broadly into abstract questions of Religion, Science, Art, and bring a finer culture to the national thought and taste." Anderson suggests that Saxon words are better suited than Latin ones to ordinary conversation, though she finds, interestingly enough, that scientists use a more Saxonized vocabulary—with the exception of technical terms—than literary writers who are trained in the classics (pp. 82-86).

Logan Pearsall Smith, American essayist and philologist who became a British subject and who wrote tracts on borrowings for the Society for Pure English, combines the arguments of Saxonists and antisaxonists. In his book *Words and Idioms* (Boston, 1925), Smith asserts that borrowing is necessary but warns that the purity of English can only be maintained if borrowed words are properly absorbed: "By the 'purity' of an English word, its homogeneity, its anglicity, we would mean then, not its Teutonic pedigree, but, whatever its source, its conformity in sound and shape with the core of the language, and its complete and satisfactory assimilation." Smith would have all borrowed terms pronounced, spelled, and inflected as if they were native English words, and he recommends that the educated classes imitate the practice of the less educated native English speakers in handling borrowed words and preserving the purity of speech (pp. 23-27).

One writer who made the unusual move of rejecting both Saxonized and borrowed words was J. Y. T. Greig, Professor of English at the University of Witwatersrand in Johannesburg. In *Breaking Priscian's Head, or English as She Will Be Spoke and Wrote* (New York, 1929), Greig, a Scot, opposed British Received Pronunciation as "that silliest and dwabliest of all the English dialects" and looked to Ireland, America, and the Commonwealth for more appropriate speech models. In addition to simplifying English grammar—Greig favored changing *does* to *do*, weakening strong verbs, replacing past participles with infinitives, and removing the distinction between the preterite and the present perfect tenses—Greig flatly states that the English language is already rich enough: "It is not actually necessary to increase the vocabulary, either by borrowing from abroad or by using native devices for word-making" (p. 69).

Otto Jespersen, the Danish linguist who was one of the most prolific writers on the English language, considered the question of borrowing in his *Growth and Structure of the English Language* (Leipzig, 1905). Sympathetic to the Saxonist point of view, Jespersen noted that there were few borrowings or loan translations in Old English, which took over from Latin only easily assimilated words, most of them concrete names, and used native terms for abstractions. Citing the example of OE *god-spell* (MnE *gospel*) 'good-speech' as a loan translation of the Greek *euangelion*, Jespersen says, "In most cases we have no such literal rendering of a foreign term, but excellent words devised exactly as if the framers of them had never heard of any foreign expression for the same conception," and he gives as examples OE *boceras* (from *boc* 'book') for *scribes*, and *heahfaeder* 'high-father' or *ealdfaeder* 'old-father' for *patriarch* (p. 45). Jespersen points out that borrowing is an unnatural linguistic process: "On the contrary, it is rather the natural thing for a language to utilize its own resources before drawing on other languages," and he adds that the modern practice of borrowing foreign vocabulary wherever possible is "out of the natural state of things" (pp. 48-49). The Anglo-Saxon word *handboc* was replaced in Middle English by the Latin *manual* and later, in the sixteenth century, the Greek term *enchiridion* was introduced. Jespersen adds, "So accustomed had the nation grown to preferring strange and exotic words that when in the nineteenth century *handbook* made its reappearance it was treated as an unwelcome intruder," and was called by Trench, in *English Past and Present* (1854), an ugly and unnecessary word scarcely fifteen years old (pp. 49-50).

Jespersen feels that English never needed classical borrowings to fill semantic gaps: "In most, perhaps in all cases, it would have been possible to find an adequate expression in the vernacular or to coin one." Unfortunately English writers began to depend on borrowings more and more: "People who had had their whole education in Latin and had thought all their best thoughts in that language to an extent which is not easy for us moderns to realize, often found it easier to write on abstract or learned subjects in Latin than in their own vernacular, and when they tried to write on these things in English, Latin words would constantly come first to their minds. Mental laziness and regard to their own momentary convenience therefore led them to retain the Latin word and give it only an English termination" (pp. 131-32).

Having explained borrowing historically and psychologically,

Jespersen accepts the existence of pairs of Saxon and Romance synonyms as affording a greater precision to English. He suggests that Latinate diction may give elegance and grandeur to poetic style, possibly because such words take more time to read or pronounce and give the reader more time for reflection and emotion. Jespersen also accepts the international intelligibility of classical terms, particularly in scientific and technological usage, but a touch of latent Saxonism comes through when he suggests that, in everyday matters, "national convenience should certainly be considered before international ease; therefore *to wire* and *a wire* are preferable to *telegraph* and *telegram.*" Jespersen also offers *wireless* as a verb as well: "Admiral N. has wirelessed that a Russian man-of-war is in sight." According to Jespersen popular names are better than learned ones "for whatever in science is not intended exclusively for the specialist. *Sleeplessness* is better than *insomnia.*" Jespersen regrets that *half-vowel* and *half-vowelish* have been replaced in linguistic terminology by *semi-vowel* and *semi-vowel-like*, and he notes that English is now being exported to other languages: "To obtain international currency a word need not have a learned appearance or be derived from Greek and Latin roots" (p. 140).

Jespersen recognizes that many loan words have become thoroughly Englished and form an indispensable part of the English vocabulary: among these are *wine, tea, bacon* and *eggs, orange* and *sugar, plunder* and *war, prison* and *judge.* But he finds that others, such as *phenomenon, diphtheria, intellectual*, and *latitudinarian* "are out of harmony with the real core or central part of the language." Jespersen feels that many loan words have no fixed pronunciation. They cannot be stressed according to English stress rules which place the accent on the root syllable, and they lead to confusion in cases where two words are similar, for example *emit* and *immit; emerge* and *immerge; illusion* and *elusion;* and *infusible*, which means either 'that may be infused or poured in' or 'incapable of being fused or melted' (p. 143).

But the worst thing about loan words, to Jespersen's mind, "is their difficulty and undemocratic character which is a natural outcome of their difficulty." Echoing Saxonists before him, Jespersen objects that "a great many [loan words] will never be used or understood by anybody that has not had a classical education," and he finds that they may contribute to the maintenance of an undemocratic society: "Their great number in the language is therefore apt to form or rather to accentuate class divisions" (p. 145). Jespersen goes on to praise those nineteenth century writers who reacted against Latinate Johnsonese, among them Tennyson and Lamb, as well as those who consciously sought to revive old and provincial words, including Coleridge, Scott, Keats, William Morris, and Swinburne.

5. CONCLUSION

In the later twentieth century the work of the Saxonists has largely been forgotten. It is true that many printed works now begin with *forewords* rather than *prefaces* and books of instruction are likely to be *handbooks* (revived *ca.* 1814) as well as *manuals*, but generally speaking the attempts to nativize the English vocabulary through purging and replacement, like most of the other attempts at reforming the English language, have failed. Despite the optimism of the Saxonists, their proposals proved at best inconsistent and unrealistic. It took hundreds of years for the English language to absorb the words that it has borrowed. It would take quite an effort to undo that work. Even more important as a cause for the movement's failure than the unworkability of the Saxonists' overall design were the Saxonisms themselves. From the sixteenth century to the twentieth the words suggested as native equivalents for borrowed terms have appeared more foreign than the terms they were designed to replace. As the prose of Barnes and of Carlyle (to take a philological and a literary example) shows, Saxon English is strange English. Its monosyllables are not necessarily transparent, and its compounds are hardly self-explaining.

The struggle between the Saxonists and their critics has left one major legacy: the stereotypical classification of Saxon words as short, tough, emotional, homespun, and concrete; and Latin words as long, flexible, cool, refined, and abstract. In the diction section of a popular contemporary writer's guide, Sheridan Baker's *The Complete Stylist and Handbook* (New York, 1980), we find an Aristotelian mixture of native and borrowed words recommended to the student:

Not too low, not too high, not too simple, not too hard an easy breadth of idea and vocabulary. English is peculiarly well endowed for this Aristotelian mixture, with the long abstract Latin words played against the short concrete Anglo-Saxon. Most of our ideas have Latin and Anglo-Saxon partners. In fact, many have a whole spectrum of synonyms from Latin through French to Anglo-Saxon, from general to specific—from *intrepidity* to *fortitude* to *valor* to *courage* to *bravery* to *pluck* to *guts*. You can choose the high word for high effect, or you can get tough with Anglo-Saxon specifics. But, again, you do not want all Anglo-Saxon, and you must especially guard against sobriety's luring you into all Latin. Tune your diction agreeably between the two extremes. [pp. 197-98]

Although he aims for a stylistic golden mean in which neither

Saxonisms nor Latinisms are to be preferred exclusively, it is clear from Baker's placement of native English words at the low end of the stylistic scale and borrowed Latinate words at the high end just who has won this particular battle of the ancients and the moderns.

NOTES

¹Cited by Basil Cottle in *The Plight of English* (New Rochelle, N.Y.: Arlington House, 1975), p. 16. The purist and archaist movements in the Renaissance, and the Saxonism that sometimes resulted from them, are discussed in J.L. Moore, *Tudor-Stuart Views on the Growth, Status, and Destiny of the English Language* (1910; rpt. College Park, Md.: McGrath, 1970); Richard Foster Jones, *The Triumph of the English Language* (Stanford, Ca.: Stanford University Press, 1953; rpt. 1966), pp. 214-71; Rosemond Tuve, "Ancients, Moderns, and Saxons," *ELH* 6 (1939): 165-90; and Charles Barber, *Early Modern English* (London: André Deutsch, 1976), pp. 76-100. The eighteenth century attitude toward archaism is briefly discussed in Susie Tucker's *Protean Shape* (London: The Athlone Press, 1967), pp. 104-13. Two useful studies of the work of William Barnes are Giles Dugdale's biography, *William Barnes of Dorset* (London: Cassell, 1953) and Willis D. Jacob's monograph, *William Barnes, Linguist, University of New Mexico Publications in Language and Literature* 9 (Albuquerque: University of New Mexico Press, 1952). And some material on Elias Molee can be found in Henry R. Stern's *The Concept of Linguistic Purity in English from 1700 to the Present* (unpublished dissertation, Northwestern University, 1968).

²Samuel Daniel, *Defence of Rhyme* (?1603), in *Elizabethan Critical Essays*, ed. G. Gregory Smith (Oxford: Oxford University Press, 1904), 2:384. George Gascoigne, *Certayne Notes of Instruction* (1575), in Smith, 1:52-53.

³Thomas Nashe, *Christs teares ouer Ierusalem* (London, 1594), pp. *2ᵛ-*3ʳ. Nashe uses archaisms as well as ornate inkhorn words, but he clearly prefers the latter and strongly defends his use of them. The economic metaphor Nashe employs is frequently used in Renaissance discussions of linguistic borrowing. Opponents of borrowing often warned of possible linguistic bankruptcy.

⁴Sir Philip Sidney, *An Apologie for Poetrie* (c. 1583), in Smith, 1:204.

⁵Richard Carew, *Epistle on the Excellency of the English Tongue* (?1595-96), in William Camden, *Remaines Concerning Britaine* (London, 1614), pp. 41-43.

⁶William Camden, *Remaines Concerning Britaine* (London, 1614), pp. 28-29.

[7]William L'Isle, *Divers Ancient Monuments in the Saxon Tongue* (London, 1638), p. E4[v].

[8]Edward Phillips, *The New World of English Words* (London, 1658), p. B4[v].

[9]E.K., *The Epistle Dedicatory to the Shepheards Calender* (1579), in Smith, 1:128-30.

[10]Richard Verstegan, *A Restitvtion of Decayed Intelligence: in antiquities* (Antwerp, 1605), pp. 204-06.

[11]*The Holy Bible: An Exact Reprint page for page of the Authorized Version Published in the year 1611* (Oxford: Oxford University Press, 1833), n.p.

[12]A.C. Partridge, *English Biblical Translation* (London: André Deutsch, 1973), p. 37.

[13]William Tyndale, trans., *The Beginning of the New Testament*, introduced by Alfred W. Pollard (Oxford: The Clarendon Press, 1926), p. xiii.

[14]Sir John Cheke, trans., *The Gospel According to Saint Matthew*, ed. James Goodwin (Cambridge, 1843), p. 13.

[15]Ralph Lever, *The Arte of Reason, Rightly Termed, Witcraft, Teaching a Perfect Way to Argue and Dispute* (London, 1573), p. v[r].

[16]John Hare, "St. Edward's Ghost" (1647; rpt. in *Harleian Miscellany* (London, 1810), 6:92-103.

[17]Nathaniel Fairfax, *A Treatise of the Bulk and Selvedge of the World* (London, 1674), pp. A3[r]-A3[v].

[18]Archibald Campbell, *Lexiphanes...Being an Attempt to Restore the English Tongue to Its Ancient Purity* (London, 1767), pp. xxii-xxiii.

[19]William Godwin, "Essay on Style," in *The Enquirer* (London, 1797), p. 478.

[20]Noah Webster, *Dissertations on the English Language* (Boston, 1789), p. 58.

[21]Lindley Murray, *An English Grammar* 2ed. (New York, 1814), 1:283.

[22]Noah Webster, *A Comprehensive Dictionary of the English Language* (Hartford, 1806), p. xvi.

[23]Thomas B. Macaulay, "John Bunyan," in *Critical, Historical, and Miscellaneous Essays and Poems* (New York: William L. Allison, 18--), 1:570.

[24]Thomas DeQuincey, "The English Language," in *The Col-*

lected Writings of Thomas DeQuincey, ed. David Masson (London, 1897), 14:149-57.

[25]Samuel K. Hoshour, *Letters to Esq. Pedant in the East, by Lorenzo Altisonant, an Emigrant to the West* (Cambridge City, Indiana, 1844), p. 12.

[26]William Barnes, "Compunds in the English Language," *Gentleman's Magazine* (1832); rpt. in Dugdale, p. 272.

[27]Jacobs, p. 32.

[28]Reviews of Barnes's *Outline of English Speech-Craft*, *Saturday Review* 46 (1878):285-86; *Athenaeum* (Aug, 17, 1878), 198-99; Archibald Ballantine, "Wardour-Street English," *Longman's Magazine* 12 (1888):585-95; rpt. in *Living Age* 179 (1888), p. 503.

[29]Elias Molee, *Plea for an American Language, or Germanic-English* (Chicago, 1888), p. 21.

[30]Elias Molee, *Pure Saxon English or, Americans to the Front* (Chicago, 1890), p. 17.

[31]Charles Louis Dessoulavy, *Word-Book of the English Tongue* (London: George Routledge and Sons, 1917), p. vii.

[32]T. L. Kington Oliphant, *The New English* (London, 1886) 2:210-34, *passim*.

[33]Herbert Thurston, "Teutonic English and Its Debasers," *The Month* 32 (1878):364.

[34]J.M.D. Meiklejohn, *The English Language, Its Grammar, History, and Literature* (Boston, 1888), pp. 127-28; 203.

[35]Charles Mackay, "The Ascertainment of English," *Nineteenth Century* 27 (1890); rpt. in *Living Age* 184 (1890): 454.

[36]Richard Burton, "The Renascence in English," *The Forum* 20 (1895): 181-92.

[37]Percy F. Bicknell, "The Retrogression in English," *The Dial* 19 (1895): 204-07. The *OED* rejects a Teutonic derivation for *massacre*.